Voices of the Second World War

Voices of the Second World War

World War

A Child's Perspective

By
Sheila Renshaw

PEN & SWORD
HISTORY

First published in Great Britain in 2017 by
Pen & Sword History
an imprint of
Pen & Sword Books Ltd
47 Church Street
Barnsley
South Yorkshire
S70 2AS

ISBN 978 1 52670 059 9

A CIP catalogue record for this book is
available from the British Library.

Printed and bound in England
By CPI Group (UK) Ltd, Croydon, CR0 4YY

Pen & Sword Books Ltd incorporates the Imprints of Pen & Sword Books
Archaeology, Atlas, Aviation, Battleground, Discovery, Family History, History,
Maritime, Military, Naval, Politics, Railways, Select, Transport, True Crime,
Fiction, Frontline Books, Leo Cooper, Praetorian Press, Seaforth Publishing,
Wharncliffe and White Owl.

For a complete list of Pen & Sword titles please contact
PEN & SWORD BOOKS LIMITED
47 Church Street, Barnsley, South Yorkshire, S70 2AS, England
E-mail: enquiries@pen-and-sword.co.uk
Website: www.pen-and-sword.co.uk

Contents

East and West 1941–1944. A boy I never knew.

When I was five and touching cowslips on the bank
Another five-year-old a thousand miles away was touching fear,

When I was six and holding fast to mother's hand
Another six-year-old a thousand miles away was torn from mother's grasp,

When I was seven and picked an apple from a tree
Another seven-year-old cried out in hungry pain,

When I was eight and sniffed the sweetness of a rose
Another eight-year-old a thousand miles away inhaled a dreadful gas,

A thousand miles along a line of latitude another boy lived out his life,
We started quits, a single cell of gratitude, the twisting strand of husband
and of wife,

The chance affair, of birthplace, east or west upon him cast a shadow, certain
dark forlorn
It chose for me life, brim full of zest, he came to dread his early eastern
dawn,

Yet men have always sought the hopeful life-giving star, our sun was ever
started in the west,
We built our churches, turned that way to pray, the ancient hope of man, the
very life of beast.

But then that other boy, a thousand miles from peace and rest might well
have said 'I wish I could have started in the west.'

David Hill,
Aged 4 years in 1939

Introduction

When war was declared in September 1939, most children in Britain and Europe were unprepared for what was going to happen. For some the war had little impact. However, two million children had their lives turned upside down when they were evacuated to places of safety. This was not always the happy picture painted by adults, these children had no idea where they were going, nor what to expect when they got there. Although some thought this might have been an exciting adventure, the reality was that they would be leaving behind all that was familiar and happy. Others had family life disrupted when fathers, older brothers and sisters left home to join the services. Some returned only occasionally on leave; many never came back.

Sometimes, part of a school was evacuated to the country, while the children who remained at home faced possible death and injury from bombing. Whenever a school was evacuated, teachers accompanied the children, giving some stability to their lives and acting as a liaison with home. This must have been a traumatic time for both children and parents. Although evacuation was not compulsory, the government tried hard to persuade parents to send their children to safety. Although some children were keen to be evacuated, the majority did not want to leave home and often had to be persuaded by their reluctant parents. Most people who opened their homes to children were kind and welcoming, but some children did not settle and remained unhappy and homesick, unable to live with strangers far from home. Parents would visit whenever they could and tried to remain positive and encouraging. Many adults did not consider the thoughts and emotions of children. It was their physical wellbeing that was of prime importance.

Younger children were encouraged to join groups such as Brownies and Wolf Cubs, where they were involved in activities such as 'collecting salvage.' This involved collecting items such as newspapers, silver paper, metal and rags. They were encouraged in their endeavours when told that any scrap metal would be turned into Spitfires.

Additionally, some groups and schools began cultivating allotments, recreation grounds and even railway sidings to grow vegetables. This all helped the 'Dig for Victory' campaign.

Some children collected the 'Hedgerow Harvest', which included berries, nuts, rose hips, nettles, sphagnum moss and other wild plants, for which the WVS (Women's Voluntary Service) paid collectors three pence a pound. Children always enjoyed playing a part in the war effort.

Older children joined Scouts, Guides, the Red Cross and the St John's Ambulance Brigade. Boys between the ages of 14 and 18 joined Army Cadets, Sea Cadets and the Air Training Corps. They were all keen to train and to contribute. Marching bands with drums and bugles could be heard at the weekends. The girls joined the Women's Junior Air Corps, the Girls' Naval Training Corps and the Girls' Training Corps, all preparing them for one of the services in the future.

Young people all over the country contributed to the war effort on the 'Home Front', often helping with harvesting and other farm work during the school holidays. Some even learnt how to drive tractors. In some cases, older children camped on the farms while the younger ones travelled out each day. Not only was this useful to the country but it gave the children a good healthy holiday and lots of fun. Some girls in the Red Cross helped in hospitals, cleaning, feeding patients and rolling bandages. Some boys acted as messengers for the ARP, the Fire Service and Home Guard, taking duty rosters and other messages to the various sites around the town. This could be dangerous, if they were caught in an air raid.

In Germany in 1933, the 'Hitler Youth' became an official government organisation and all children with an Aryan or pure German background were forced to join from the age of 10. Children with any Jewish blood were not allowed. It was very popular with most children as it offered many exciting activities such as camping, hiking, singing, eating around campfires and marching with bands. Hitler was keen to win the minds of children and to prepare them for his future dreams. He saw himself as the Father and Protector of his people and took every opportunity to visit, talk and to encourage children to be proud Germans

At the very beginning of the war Britain realised that it was necessary to introduce food rationing, so that everyone would get a fair share of basic foods. Ration books were issued in January 1940; children under the age of 6 had a green ration book and, after a while, older children were issued with blue ones. In general, they received fewer rations than adults, but were allowed extra milk and welfare foods such as cod liver oil and fruit juice. In 1942, sweet rationing was introduced and some chocolate manufacturers actually made small chocolate bars. These were not as popular as the small sweets in big glass jars on display in the shops. Tiny sweets such as 'Hundreds and Thousands', and orange and lemon pips were the most popular. They would go a long way.

Lord Woolton, the Minister for Food, was determined that all children would receive an appropriate diet to keep them fit and strong. He decided that children under the age of 5 would receive a pint of milk each day. In 1942, schoolchildren were given a free bottle of milk each day. To help parents provide interesting and nourishing meals, the Ministry of Food and several women's magazines provided recipes and tips for preparing satisfying meals with the limited food available.

Families were encouraged to grow fruit and vegetables and to keep chickens and rabbits to supplement the rations. This was quite easy as the rabbits and chickens were easy to look after; a problem arose however, when the animals were to be killed. Many people just could not kill them and many children vowed they would not, in any circumstances, eat a pet. Fish was not rationed and fish and chip shops were always open for business.

I have interviewed each contributor personally, both in this country and abroad. All were happy to talk about their experiences and to share their memories. I have tried to record their stories as accurately as possible. This book allows us to share some of the memories of these people, all different, both here in the UK and abroad, yet everything is connected in its own way. It shows that in war everyone is involved: men, women and children. The ages of the children ranged from 2 years old to the teenage years. At the beginning of the war some lived in Britain, others lived in Russia, Germany, Netherlands, Norway and other parts of Europe. Their stories are very different. There were children who hardly knew there was a war raging throughout Europe, whereas others lived through deprivation, starvation and danger in the towns and cities. Most children grew up very quickly and accepted responsibility. Boys took over many of the jobs their absent fathers had done and girls helped their mothers in the home. Many boys found the war exciting and enjoyed looking for souvenirs, pieces of crashed aeroplanes, shrapnel, shell and rocket cases and any other items that had fallen from the sky.

Some children however, were witness to some horrific events that have remained with them all their lives.

I have thought about writing this book for several years, but recently decided that if I did not write it now, the stories would be lost forever. I feel the stories must be recorded and remembered as they are important memories of a critical period in the twentieth century. I have been privileged to be able to talk to these people and hope that you will enjoy reading their very personal accounts.

Chapter 1

Sheila – 5 years old: Outer Hebrides, Scotland

When war was declared in 1939, I was living with my parents at Sealand, an RAF station on the north coast of Wales.

I was not aware of soldiers, barrage balloons, air raid shelters or any of the other preparations for war. I was at school at the local convent, and this was the most important thing in my life. I loved being there; as an only child, it gave me the opportunity to play with other children.

Early one morning in 1940, we were lined up and everyone was given a gas mask in a brown cardboard box. From then on, every morning a whistle would blow and we would go to the cloakroom, get our gas masks, line up in twos and go down to the cellar. This was a large room with benches all around. We put on our gas masks, sat down on the nearest bench and remained like this until the whistle blew again. Then we were allowed to take them off and go back to the classroom with our teachers. There was no running, rushing or pushing allowed, we just had to do things quietly and to keep calm. To begin with, some of the children hated this and cried, but our teacher always helped them and they soon got used to the routine.

In 1941, my parents decided that it would be safer for me to go to stay with my grandparents and a great aunt on the Isle of Lewis in the Outer Hebrides. Being in the RAF, my father knew that he could move to other potentially perilous flying stations. Also, Liverpool was fairly close to where we lived and it had already experienced some really severe bombing raids.

My mother and I left our home late one evening and travelled by train through the night, passing through Liverpool in the middle of a massive air raid, seeing searchlights making a pattern in the sky, searching for enemy aircraft. There were flashes and lights everywhere and a deep orange glow on the horizon. We were totally unaware of the devastation being caused around us and of course, the loss of life. Years later, I discovered that we had actually travelled on one of the worst nights of the Liverpool Blitz.

The next day we passed through the Highlands with its impressive scenery. Dotted here and there were Highland cattle with their huge horns, and deer roaming the steep hills. This was an entirely new experience for me. I had never seen mountains, large spaces, lochs, Highland cattle or deer before.

We took the ferry from the Kyle of Lochalsh to Stornoway and crossed The Minch. Years later, I heard that the captain of the ferry had no idea that mines had been laid the day before.

I was to spend the next five years with grandparents I did not know, but they were welcoming, loving and kind. It must have been quite a challenge for them, to suddenly have a young child to look after.

We lived in a small village called Sandwich, on the outskirts of Stornoway. The village consisted mainly of crofts. Most islanders kept chickens and grew fruit and vegetables but quite a few reared cows, sheep and pigs. Every morning, I would go to the farm next door to collect milk. They made butter and cheese from surplus milk and they always gave me some to take home as a special treat. They allowed me to churn the butter and feed the chickens. People on the island bartered produce, which certainly helped to supplement their rations.

However, all items such as coffee, tea, tinned goods and dried goods, such as oatmeal had to be shipped across from the mainland, therefore these items were always in short supply. Quite often the shelves in the local store were almost empty. Stornoway had a small fishing fleet that went out in the evenings to catch herring and any other fish that was available. Most of the herring were turned into wonderful kippers in smoke houses and sent to the mainland. There was no shortage of fish for people to buy and fortunately, fish was cheap and was not rationed.

I was very happy at the village primary school where my aunt was the deputy head. I soon made friends with the local children and when I acquired a Hebridean accent I was accepted. Occasionally my parents came up to the islands. This was a time of great excitement for everyone. It was difficult for service people to get leave and my father had a very busy job.

The school was a completely different experience for me. When a child misbehaved, he or she was struck on the hand with a leather strap in front of the class. Even children as young as 5 were given this horrid punishment, which was very painful. I only experienced it once but I have never forgotten it and have always been against any form of physical violence against children.

All the younger children wrote and did their arithmetic on slates. This continued until we were able to form the letters and numbers correctly. Then we were given an exercise book. We had to take great care of these books as paper was in short supply and, like so many other goods, had to be brought in by ship.

A very large air raid shelter was built in the playground. The children all collected newspaper as part of helping the war effort and, by the end of the war, the shelter was absolutely full of paper and was never emptied. Every week children brought more paper which was carefully stacked. It did not occur to anyone that we might be bombed and have need of the shelter. We seemed so far away from the war.

The Hebrides did not appear to be affected by the war at all. There were no barrage balloons, guns, soldiers or shelters in gardens. However, the parents and brothers of many of my friends had gone away to fight and there were only a few older men around. Certainly, there were no young men to be seen.

Boys and girls returned from school at the end of the day and helped their mothers with work on the farms and crofts, feeding the animals and milking cows. I often went next door to see if I could help. They were very kind and they always found a job for me.

In the summer holidays, older boys and girl rounded up cows from the various crofts and took all of them to graze on the cliff tops, where it was particularly good pasture land. I was always pleased when they took me along because it seemed like an adventure. We were never aware of any danger with the cows near the edge of the cliffs. We took sandwiches with us and collected water from a well. At this time I visited my grandfather, who was the lighthouse keeper. I remember climbing up the many steps of the spiral staircase to the top of the lighthouse where there was a most wonderful view of sea and sky. Nearby, we spent time picking wild raspberries and tayberries, some of which were eaten and occasionally there enough left to take home.

One commodity that was always in short supply was coal, this had to be brought in by ship from the mainland. However, the islanders burned peat. In late summer, families would go out to the moors to cut this and bring it home on a horse drawn cart. I think it was common land and each family had an area they could work. The cutting and harvesting of peat was hard work but children helped by stacking it carefully and loading the cart. Travelling, sitting on top of the load on the back of the cart was exciting. We arrived home dirty, tired and hungry.

When not at school, we were allowed to play on the sandy beaches close to the village. One day we were playing, when one of my friends saw an aircraft approaching, flying very low. It flew overhead at great speed and then shot bullets into the sand. We could see German markings on the side of the plane and the pilot in the cockpit. It then flew back over us, repeating the firing. Then he flew away. Quite an experience! We then looked for the bullets and took them home as souvenirs. Nobody believed our story until we showed them the bullets and told everyone how we had all just escaped certain death!

Another extraordinary story was told to me by my grandfather. Stornoway was the main fishing port on the island and it had a good deep harbour. Before the war it was quite normal for Dutch, German and French fishing boats to visit the islands. Their crews came ashore and made friends with the locals in the various pubs. On one particular day in 1943, a young man came into the only hotel and was enjoying a whisky when one of the local men thought he recognised him. He expressed surprise but the young man told him he was part of the Free Dutch Navy. But the landlord was suspicious and called the police who came and arrested him. It transpired that the man was, in fact, the captain of a German U boat! He had come ashore, leaving the submarine out of sight in a local creek. The Royal Navy soon arrived and captured his U boat and all its crew. They were transported to a prisoner of war camp for the duration of the war!

Towards the end of the war, an airfield was built on the north side of the island and life changed for everyone. Until then, cars were rarely seen, as only a few people were entitled to petrol. Most people walked or rode bicycles or travelled on the weekly bus. We no longer played on the roads or sledged on them in winter, it all became too dangerous.

At the beginning of 1945, my father who was, by then, based in Algiers, flew up to Stornoway and brought with him two huge bunches of bananas, enough for every child in the school to have one, a rare treat indeed! I did not realise he was coming, so it was quite a shock to see him in his uniform Most of us could not remember ever seeing or eating a banana before. It was such a luxury.

In 1944 my sister was born in Epsom, during an air raid. A flying bomb exploded in the grounds of the maternity home and my mother and sister were blown out through a glass door, ending up in the garden. Fortunately, they were not injured although they were covered with glass. Even to this day, my sister is sensitive to any loud noise or explosion.

On VE Day there was a big party for all the school, with tables and chairs put out in the playground. Parents brought food and drink and we ended up playing games. In the evening, we went to a church hall where there was more food and drink, followed by a ceilidh with music and dancing for children and adults alike. Everyone seemed so happy and relaxed. It had been a very long war. I was so lucky to have had a happy time, where my education was not disrupted and I was well cared for, loved and protected. I returned to my parents once the war was over and soon found myself living in Algiers and Egypt. I went from living on a wet and windy island to the burning heat of Algiers.

I think my time on the islands prepared me well for my future life and I always look back on it with fond memories. The schooling I received gave me a good start and prepared me for Grammar School when we returned from the Middle East several years later.

Sheila lives in the South of England with her husband, two daughters, three grandchildren and a great grandchild. She was commissioned in the WRAF and then trained as a teacher.

Chapter 2

Derek – 9 years old: Hull, England

Even before war was declared there was fear of bombing and invasion. I remember hearing the prime minister's announcement at 11 o'clock on the morning of Sunday 3 September, saying that we were at war with Germany. From that moment, life changed for everybody.

My parents had lived through the First World War and they still had terrible memories of that time. There was anxiety everywhere. The newspapers and the BBC news gave the latest reports of what was happening in Europe. It all seemed to be bad news. Air raid shelters were being built as quickly as possible, some in gardens, some in the streets and some as indoor shelters. Sirens could be heard from time to time to check the warning system. Advance notice was given but I will never forget that wailing sound. Barrage balloons filled the sky. When a raid was imminent, all the balloons were raised to a great height. One day, I saw at least ten of them struck by lightning, with their hydrogen burning, producing great fireballs in the sky. This was followed by steel cables falling, causing damage to chimneys and buildings and injuries to people below.

One night, an RAF aircraft ran into a balloon cable and crashed into a house two doors away from where we lived. I will never forget the sound of the explosion. Because I was so young I did not think of the airmen who perished.

Gas masks were delivered to families and fitted by an Air Raid Warden, in my case it was my father.

I hated the idea of gas masks and found the experience quite claustrophobic. I can remember my father insisting that I put it on and left it on for some time.

As a family, we listened to the BBC news and the stirring speeches by Winston Churchill. My parents realised that the nearby docks and industry were prime targets for the bombers so they decided that I should be evacuated. Some of my friends had already been sent to their relatives in the country.

I attended the Marist College in Hull, a boys' school with very strict discipline. Arrangements were made for seventy of us to travel by train to

Holme-on-Spalding-Moor, a village twenty-five miles away. There were seventy boys in school uniform with their bags and gas masks, each one with a large luggage label attached, showing name and address. I can remember walking down the platform at Paragon station with my friends from school and a few of our teachers. On the train we sat quietly watching the Yorkshire countryside go by. Suddenly it did not seem so much like an adventure. I was homesick already. I asked if I could stay on a farm but was put into a primitive cottage. At night, I saw the flashes of bombs and guns and the orange glow in the sky from fires in Hull. I was lonely, very homesick and worried about my parents.

The cottage had no running water. Four cottages shared one old pump and there was no electricity or gas. There was a paraffin lamp for lighting, and cooking was done on an old coal-fired stove. The only toilet was at the bottom of the long garden, quite frightening if one had to go out at night in the dark, sometimes in deep snow. What a change from my comfortable life at home.

However, after a few weeks, I was transferred to a friendly billet. This was owned by a retired art mistress, a very strict Italian lady called Miss Matzinger. She was kind, fed me well and looked after me. She showed interest in my drawings and actually took me out and bought paper, pencils and paints for me, I was so pleased with these. She encouraged me to paint and draw and gave me confidence in my ability, which turned out to be very useful later in life. However, if I was late for a meal, she was standing at the door with a cane in her hand. Thankfully she never used it.

All the evacuees attended the village school, although we were taught separately from the village children. Some of our lessons were in a small village hall. Most of our teachers were Catholic Fathers who came from our main school in Hull. It was not a friendly village and we did not mix with the local children.

During the holidays, a lorry driver took me with him each day to a local airfield which was under construction. We had to unload thousands of bricks, which was great fun but really hard work. There were no wages for this job.

When the Wellington and Whitley bombers arrived on the completed airfield, I spent hours standing at the end of the runway watching them land, take off and being loaded with bombs. They flew right over my head. It was so exciting!

One thing I did not appreciate was that fast German bombers occasionally attacked airfields at low level, so danger was never far away. At this time, something occurred which was to bring about a major change in my life.

I and two other boys decided to place coins, stones and then a half a brick on the main railway line between York and Hull. We just wanted to see what would happen. This idea came from a film we had seen in the village hall.

When the train hit our brick, there was a cloud of red dust and we ran. The train made an emergency stop at the next station where a shaken driver reported the incident to the police. It took the police three weeks to identify the culprits. Fortunately for us our headmaster was given the option of dealing with us. A public caning was arranged and this punishment was witnessed by the whole school, on the stage in the village school. The people in the village soon heard about this, including Miss Matzinger, who immediately wrote to my mother. In the first line she said: 'Will you please remove your son from my house at once?' The words 'at once' were underlined in black ink.

My mother came and tried to arrange another billet but, much to my delight, nobody wanted me. So, it was back to the excitement of the air raids and my friends in Hull. We were really sorry to have caused so much worry to so many people.

I returned to my old school, cycling three miles there and back, twice every day. This was the time of daylight air raids by fast, low-flying aircraft. If the sirens sounded, my father told me to rush to the nearest house and ask for shelter. Sometimes these aircraft arrived without warning.

The sirens sounded most nights but we usually went to bed as normal in the house and then, went downstairs as quickly as possible to the air raid shelter in the garden.

My father, as an air raid warden, had to ensure that no lights were show-ing in the area and, when bombs fell nearby, he helped to rescue the victims and to extinguish the many fires started by incendiary bombs. My friends and I helped him to give public demonstrations on how to extinguish them.

Sometimes, during a raid, there would be a lull and we would leave the shelter and stand in the garden, watching the many searchlights sweeping from side to side, looking for German aircraft. On one occasion my father suggested we should go and look for mushrooms in a field behind our garden! The searchlights sweeping the sky gave enough light for us to spot them. Suddenly, at the top of a cone of searchlights, we spotted a tiny Heinkel 111 at a great height, lit up like a sparkling jewel. We ran as fast as we could for our shelter with guns firing and salvos of rockets being launched from all around. Shrapnel and shell cases were soon falling on to roofs and dustbins. The noise was incredible. My mother was really worried when we returned to the shelter! Next day, I discovered an unexploded incendiary bomb that had lodged deep in the lawn, just 3ft from our shelter.

One day, at school, the siren sounded, so we ran across the playground to the school shelter. At that moment, we heard the noise of an aircraft overhead. We stopped and looked up to see a German bomber in a vertical dive with a Spitfire on its tail, firing its guns. All the boys were cheering. At the last moment, the German pulled out of the dive and shot across the city at very low level and high speed. Fortunately, the pilot did not fly into any of the many barrage balloon cables. We heard later that the aircraft had been shot down on the banks of the River Humber and that the crew had survived.

In the evenings, we tuned into broadcasts in English from Germany. We often heard 'Lord Haw Haw' (William Joyce, the traitor) broadcasting. One evening he said that the five chimneys on the large power station in Hull, close to where we lived, would not be there in the morning. That night, there was a heavy raid but the chimneys were still there at the end of the war.

Whenever possible, I cycled to an RAF station ten miles away and stood at the end of the runway to watch Spitfires take off and land. Young pilots were training to fly these advanced aircraft. It was always so exciting to watch them trying to do a good landing. Frequently, an airman fired a red flare to advise the pilots to 'go round again'. On more than one occasion, the flare landed in a cornfield and started a fire very close to where I was standing. Very quickly fire engines appeared and tried to minimise the damage, they were kept busy all day.

I was lucky that my father did not have to go to war, as he was over the age of 39. His firm changed from making domestic products such as Brasso, washing materials, metal tins, etc. to aeroplane parts. Like many men, he worked a twelve-hour day, six days a week. Some nights he returned to the factory for fire-watching duties. This was a very long day. At weekends, he reported to the nearby Wardens' depot, which was alongside a barrage balloon launching site. Sometimes I managed to persuade him to take me with him.

I joined the school section of the Air Training Corps, giving a false age. We met once a week and was eventually given a uniform. We learnt about the RAF, aircraft recognition, meteorology and air navigation. My prize possession was a large chart of the silhouettes of both German and English aircraft. This had pride of place on my bedroom wall.

I went to summer camps with the school ATC. We were billeted in Nissen huts and had great fun. My first flight was from Brough, on the Humber, in the front seat of a Tiger Moth. I found it so exciting with the ground passing by so quickly when we were taking off, followed by some aerobatics. During a summer camp I had three flights in Wellington bombers. It was surprising that this was allowed, as we were still at war. At that time, the Wellingtons were used as target practice for Spitfires, using camera guns. There had been a collision between a Wellington and a Spitfire on an exercise only a few days before, with fatal results for all those involved. On another occasion, I went up in a Dakota on a test flight after it had had a service on one of its engines. When we took off the engine failed immediately! The pilot did a tight turn on the one good engine, but could only attempt a forced landing on a runway, which was being rebuilt at the time. As we landed, I remember seeing workmen running for their lives, throwing their tools away. We just missed two cement mixers, rollers and other equipment. The incident was in that evening's paper. We had a lucky escape, but it was then that I decided that one day, I would fly with the RAF, as a pilot. The die was cast.

In Hull, there was a street that had been badly bombed. Eventually the few remaining residents were moved away and the army used it to train soldiers in street fighting. The noise of explosions and machine-gun fire could be heard across the city. Soldiers went from one house to another fighting in preparation for D-day. Bren machine guns fired live ammunition, and Thunder Flashes were used to simulate grenades. It was very noisy and smoke was everywhere but, for a boy, it was a very exciting place to be. One afternoon I was very late for school. I just could not pull myself away from such an exciting scene!

We often played war games on bomb sites, quite unaware of the dangers of unexploded bombs.

The war eventually came to an end. VE and VJ days were celebrated by everyone. There was great merriment on the field behind our house and in all the city streets. Tables and chairs were brought out, people ate, drank and enjoyed themselves. For everyone there was a great sense of relief, after five and a half years. Street lights were on again and blackout curtains taken down, never to be used again.

It was then the time to wait for friends, families and loved ones to return. In our local area some came back wounded and others never returned. It took some time for houses to be rebuilt and rationing to end.

For me, the war had been a time of great adventures.

A few years later Derek did achieve his dream and flew with the RAF as a pilot for twenty years, continuing his exciting early life.

He now lives in the South of England with his wife. He has two daughters, three grandchildren and a great grandchild.

Chapter 3

Nadia – 14 years old: Ukraine (USSR)

So that we can understand Nadia's story, I have to start before the war began. Nadia lived in a little village called Chernihov in the Ukraine, about 100 miles north of Kiev. In those days, it was part of Russia (USSR). Schooling for most children ended at the age of 14, but the headmaster of the local village school suggested to Nadia's parents that she should carry on with her studies, in a college in Kharkov. This school specialised in preparing students for a career in medicine. Nadia passed the entrance exam and started on her course, some 300 miles from home. It was a long overnight train journey to get to Kharkov. She rented a mattress to put on the wooden benches.

Now we hear Nadia's story.

When I arrived at the college in Kharkov, in September 1939, I was 14 years old. It was all very exciting and I was looking forward to starting my course. We were aware that Germany had invaded Poland, but Stalin had broadcast to the people that the USSR had signed a pact with Hitler and there was no need for concern. He told us that the USSR was a powerful nation with a large army, far stronger than any possible invading force. This turned out to be far from the truth.

At the same time as these broadcasts, we children – girls, boys, women and any men who were available, were given spades and told to dig anti-tank trenches. The trenches were very wide. The idea was, that a tank would go in nose first and not be able to get out. In fact, when the Germans did arrive and realised the tactics, they put temporary bridges over the trenches so that the tanks could pass over easily.

For the first few months, nothing much happened and life seemed fairly normal. I was really enjoying my studies and I wrote regularly to my brother who also had a scholarship and was studying in St Petersburg. I was worried about my family as it was very difficult to get any news from home. Before long, one could not even send a letter as post offices and postal services had closed down. The village of Chernihov was too isolated to have a telephone, so it was not possible to contact them in any way.

Children were not evacuated, as there was nowhere safe for them to go. However, some families left and tried to reach the safety of relatives in the country. One of these was our teacher and his family. They put all their precious furniture onto a large cart and left. Unfortunately, they were robbed by a band of thieves. They returned to their flat empty-handed, having lost everything. At least, it was lucky that it had not been taken over by squatters. Everyone had been told that if you left your house or flat you must leave your key in the lock, so that the door would not be damaged if someone came looking for shelter. We were taught that we must always respect authority and follow instructions.

One day at the end of lessons, our headmaster said that the school was closing that evening and we were all to go home. He had heard that the German army was approaching the Ukraine. Girls who lived locally packed up and left. My friend and I packed and went to the railway station to see if we could get home. It was full of people, young, old and even soldiers, all trying to get on a train. We stayed for a little while, but most trains were passing through full of soldiers and not stopping. Those that did stop were so full that we could not get on. There were people hanging on to the top and outside of the train. It was a frightening picture. There was no way of knowing where the trains were going or where they had come from. Nobody had any answers.

We then decided it would be safer if we stayed together and remain where we were for the time being. We could not risk starting the journey only to be thrown off the train in some unknown, isolated place. This would have been a very dangerous situation. We had both started at the college at the same time and came from nearby villages.

We found that all our teachers had left the school and we were totally on our own. Most of them were Jewish and wanted to get as far away from the Germans as possible. They had heard about the persecution of Jews in Poland and Czechoslovakia and there were rumours about concentration camps. We went to the hospital that was next door to our school, saw the matron and told her about our situation. We asked her if we could stay for a while and help in the hospital. Fortunately, she agreed and said that we could stay with her for the time being in her very pleasant little cottage in the hospital grounds.

We were young and healthy, they needed people to help and we needed some safety. There was always plenty of work to do and not enough regular staff available. We were given some basic instruction and then we got on with work, cleaning, washing patients, rolling bandages etc. It was decided that if patients were fit enough, they could go home or they would be sent to a convalescent hospital. However, some cases had to remain as they were too ill to move.

Fortunately, in the basement of the hospital we had cold storage and there was quite a lot of food down there, including dried food, smoked and preserved meat and fish and vegetables. We also had extensive vegetable and fruit gardens, some goats and a cow. We transferred all the patients to one ward so that we could keep them warm and comfortable.

We heard on the wireless that the Germans were advancing but rumours were everywhere and we really did not know what to expect, or believe. We heard terrible stories about how they treated Ukrainians, Russians and other Eastern Europeans. All our news, however, came from Russian broadcasts.

By this time, all the officials had deserted the town and, consequently, there was no law any more. People were frightened and desperate. They broke into stores and looted everything they could find, especially sacks of flour and anything else they could get hold of. The shops had very little left and the shelves were empty because, by this time, there were no deliveries into the town.

The hospital was a very grand building, built in the time of Tsarist Russia. It was in large, beautiful grounds far away from everyday problems. It was surrounded by a tall stone wall and had large gates. Before being turned into a hospital, it had been the summer palace for one of the Tsar's children.

One morning we were working when we heard the terrific noise of vehicles, tanks and shouting soldiers nearby. We looked out of the window and, coming across the grass towards the building, were tanks, armoured cars and soldiers everywhere. The Germans had arrived. We were petrified and gathered together in one ward. The soldiers crashed into the room, pointing guns at us. I am not sure who looked the most frightened, the German soldiers or the nurses. The soldiers did not know what to expect. They had heard that the hospital was full of Russian soldiers. What they did not know was that all the soldiers had left several days earlier and they had retreated towards Moscow, not stopping to fight.

A sergeant was in the front, shouting at us in German. He sounded very angry and thought that if he shouted loud enough, we would understand him. After a few minutes, I decided to act. I had learnt German at school so I stepped forward and said, 'If you stop shouting, I will tell you what our names are and what you want to know'. He was speechless and instantly changed his attitude. How could I, an ignorant Russian girl, '*untermenschen*' (subhuman) speak and understand German? I spoke in my schoolgirl German: 'I am a schoolgirl but I can speak and can understand some

German'. I told him he was in a hospital. Then the door opened and an officer in a splendid uniform came in carrying a revolver. I tried to tell him we
were just looking after sick people. Another older man said he was a doctor
and they were going to use our hospital for wounded German soldiers. He
said they would transfer all civilian patients to another hospital. We never
found out where they went or what had happened to them. Even to this day
I think about them. He told us that we were to remain in the hospital as we
were needed for work. He also said I could help them as an interpreter. For
the next few weeks I spent more time interpreting than nursing on the wards
and my German improved rapidly. A university student called Wanda was
also brought to the hospital to officially interpret from Russian or Ukrainian
to German. We were both kept very busy. The Germans brought women in
from the neighbourhood to do some menial tasks, such as cleaning, washing
bed linen and preparing vegetables.

Eventually, German army nursing sisters came into the hospital to take
charge. They looked so smart in their long grey dresses, white aprons and
long grey cloaks with red lining. We all thought they looked wonderful. On
the whole, they treated us well but we were very aware that they were in
charge and we had to do all the basic jobs. We were all kept very busy. My
main job was to wash the wounded soldiers who came in very dirty with
open wounds and, in some cases, in a poor condition. Stretcher-bearers
brought in wounded soldiers with so many different types of wounds and
burns. Some of them were so badly injured they were not even aware of what
we were doing for them. There were several different nationalities fighting
alongside the Germans, so our patients included Hungarians, Romanians,
Latvians and many more. The doctors were very efficient and worked very
long hours and expected us to do the same. They brought medicines with
them we had never seen before, mainly to fight against infection. Until then
more patients died of infection rather than from their wounds or injuries.

We were like prisoners, too terrified to go out of the hospital grounds.
We were warned that if anyone was caught outside, they would be robbed,
attacked and possibly raped by local Ukrainians. It was much safer inside.
We also heard that if the Germans found any girls outside they would be
sent to Germany as slaves. It was a very frightening time. We never knew
what was going to happen and just had to do as we were told. Most Germans
thought all eastern Europeans were uneducated.

One evening when I had finished work and was going off duty, I was
summoned to the Officers' Mess by the surgeon I worked alongside. All
the officers were sitting around a table and had just finished their meal.

My doctor called me to him and told me to sit down. I wondered what I had done wrong. Sitting opposite him was a very young SS officer. He was incredibly handsome with blond hair and blue eyes. My doctor said to me 'Nadia this young officer does not believe a young Russian girl can be educated'. The SS officer stood up, came round and handed me a book in German by Proust and said 'read that,' I stood up and the doctor told me to sit down, he said 'Nadia, you are not in school now'. I read half a page, then he told me to translate it into Russian. This I did, then he asked me what the paragraph meant. I said that I had not studied Proust, so therefore could not give an educated explanation. The other doctors around the table applauded and the SS officer looked displeased. He said that he was amazed that I was educated at all and could actually understand a book in German. He had a proposition for me, I could leave the hospital and work in a hotel entertaining German officers; I would be paid, have good food and nice clothes. I was frightened and asked the colonel if I was being forced to do this. He just said to the lieutenant 'I am sorry but I rely on Nadia in theatre. My work is of the utmost importance to the Third Reich, I am trying to save the lives of German soldiers so they can return to their regiments.' My doctor thanked me and told me I could go back to my quarters. When I got back to my room I was still shaking, my friend said I had a lucky escape; if I had agreed, I would have been a prostitute.

The colonel was in command of the hospital, he was always kind and polite and seemed to appreciate all our hard work. That had been a terrifying moment as I did not know what was happening and everyone was frightened of the SS, they were totally unpredictable and fanatical. Nobody ever mentioned this incident again.

One of the worst things for me was not being able to contact my family to let them know where I was and that I was still alive. I had left my mother behind with three younger brothers to look after. I knew my father had been sent to the Urals to work in a factory making tanks, and my elder brother was now in the Red Army. I knew that we had a cow, some pigs and chickens and a plot of land to cultivate at home. We were part of a collective farm, so I felt sure they would be able to survive. There were no shops in the village, but neighbours were able to barter surplus produce.

In 1942, German farmers came and settled in the Ukraine, taking over and running the collective farms with the idea that the Ukraine would eventually become part of Germany. They came with the authority of the SS, so no one dared to challenge them. They then sent most of the food they cultivated either to Germany or to their front line.

Trains came from Germany full of hand machinery and returned with anything they could find, food, wheat, animals and vegetables. Some trains even took rich topsoil from the Ukraine to replace the soil in Germany. By this time everyone was starving. In Europe, people would eat anything that was available, even tree bark. Fortunately, at the hospital, the Germans fed the staff and patients. They needed us to do the work, so they had to feed us. In the grounds we grew as much fruit and vegetables as we could. We also had chickens and a cow and some goats for milk.

The routine continued. More and more badly injured soldiers were brought to the hospital, all needing constant attention. We were not allowed a wireless or newspapers, so any news was by word of mouth, some true, some fanciful. We did not even know about the siege of Stalingrad. Everything was hearsay. As time went on, many patients died from their wounds. We just could not save them as medical supplies were depleted and nothing was being replaced.

It eventually became apparent that the Germans were retreating and the Red Army was advancing. At this stage, only very badly injured patients were admitted. One morning, we were told that we had to pack up all our things as quickly as we could. We were taken to the railway station with the injured soldiers and put on a train, heading towards Germany. We had no choice as to what to do. The soldiers needed us to look after them for the journey ahead. We thought we might be able to escape from the train, but we had no money and no papers. After two long days, we arrived at Zilena, where a field hospital had been established. When we arrived we could see rows and rows of tents that looked like a barracks.

English and American planes flew overhead. One American plane was shot down and four of the aircrew were brought in with broken bones. We looked after these young men. One was Jewish and fortunately, could speak some German and also Yiddish, which is similar, so we were able to communicate. The Germans did not realise he was Jewish, otherwise they may have shot him.

The Russians were approaching and we were told that, if we were captured and they discovered we had worked for the Germans, we would be sent to a Gulag (a concentration camp) in Siberia. A fate worse than death! Once again we did not know what to do.

One morning, a German doctor came in and said 'you are on your own now, it is every man for himself. The Russians will be here soon, so I suggest you head for the West as quickly as possible.' There was chaos and a great deal of fear everywhere. The German soldiers were certainly afraid of being taken prisoner by advancing Russians who would show no mercy.

We managed to get several lifts with the soldiers who were trying to get to Italy, so they could surrender to the British. Every now and then, we were put off a truck to make room for more German soldiers. For part of the journey, we were even on a troop train. We hoped that, if we went with the soldiers, we would end up in a POW camp and become 'displaced persons'. It seemed to be the only sensible choice.

Going through Yugoslavia was difficult and dangerous. We were aware that we could be attacked at any time by a Partisan unit whose main aim was to destroy convoys and rid their country of Germans. We just knew we had to get to the West. There were retreating soldiers everywhere. Usually, the lorries stopped and the soldiers gave us a lift. There were only a few girls on the move and we were in uniform. We had no money and nowhere to go.

Early one morning, we were being driven very carefully on a mountain road when, to our amazement, coming towards us was a convoy travelling in the opposite direction. We were so relieved to discover it was full of British soldiers. The German soldiers immediately surrendered and we were escorted to a temporary camp for PoWs. We discovered we were now actually in Italy.

The British treated us well and gave us food and drink and a warm billet. A Red Cross lady gave us clothes to look through and told us to select what we wanted. Unfortunately, most of the clothes were for children! A few days later, we were interviewed by a young British officer.

Through an Italian interpreter he asked us where we had come from and what we had we been doing. I told him we were from the Ukraine, and had been nursing wounded German soldiers. I explained how we had been stranded at school, unable to return to our families and that now we would like to train as nurses. He agreed that it would be dangerous for us to return to the Ukraine. He said we would be able find work in England and he would personally recommend it. He was true to his word and, after several months in the camp, we arrived in Southampton on a rainy morning. What intense relief; we were safe at last, in England. It all seemed very strange, but everyone was kind and willing to help. Our first and most important job was to learn to speak English as nobody in England could speak Russian and it was suggested that we should not speak German.

Many years later, in 1968, I returned to the Ukraine to meet up once again with my mother, father and three brothers. It was such a very happy reunion. They had lived through a very difficult time, even living through the Germans' 'scorched earth policy'. They had survived and had been able to rebuild their lives.

It was only after the war that I heard about the atrocities that had been committed as the German Army advanced into Russia, followed by the SS. It was then that we heard about the concentration camps and mass killings. During the war, the camps were just rumours that we dared not mention. Somehow, we had managed to survive all that.

My war was full of traumatic experiences and very hard work. We were never sure that we would survive and we never knew what would happen next. However, I am sure that it was the initial kindness of the matron who allowed us to stay with her and to work in her hospital that saved our lives.

Nadia trained in London and became a State Registered Nurse. Her friend emigrated to Canada where she also trained as a nurse.

Nadia now lives in the South of England. She is a widow with two married sons and many grandchildren and great grandchildren.

Chapter 4

Val – 5 years old: Coventry, England

I was 5½ years old when war was declared; I lived in Coventry with my parents and two teenage sisters. I remember playing in the garden when a neighbour called to tell us that she had just heard that we were at war with Germany. Although I did not understand what that meant, I realised it must be something serious as both my mother and her friend were upset and crying.

My father was too old to be called up so he worked in a factory making aeroplane parts. In the evening, he went out again on duty as an air raid warden. For a few months all was quiet. Air raid shelters were built, barrage balloons were raised and lowered and every now and then, air raid sirens could be heard. I hated the large silver balloons which seemed so menacing and the loud wailing sound of the sirens frightened me.

I was at school at St Joseph's Convent, which was evacuated to Stoneleigh Abbey, a fantastic country manor house with large grounds, huge trees and flowering bushes. I found it very different from life in a busy city.

We slept on camp beds in the ballroom and were given navy blue blankets. I was fortunate enough to have my bed by the window and was allowed to put my teddies on the windowsill. I had always been afraid of the nuns. Although they were kind, their dark brown habits frightened me, so I was delighted to find that the teacher who was sleeping with us was our music teacher and not a nun. She was very kind and would comfort all the children who were homesick and explained why we had to be there. Fortunately, most of the children adapted to the situation fairly quickly.

My mother and sisters visited me regularly. On one occasion they came with my uncle in his car. Before they left, we were all crying and they realised how unhappy I was and how I just wanted to go home. My mother eventually agreed that I could go back with them. She said that if we were going to be killed, at least we would all be together. We then found out that there were no spare places at the local school in Coventry. My mother taught me until the end of term and then I went to Stoke National C of E School.

Before the Germans started bombing, my father had built an Anderson shelter in the garden. Whenever the sirens sounded, we went into it as quickly as we could, taking food and drink just in case we were there for a long time. It always felt cold and damp even though we had a paraffin heater.

One night my mother fell asleep in the shelter and she woke up with a headache feeling sick. I can remember waking up lying on the garden path being very sick. This had been caused by fumes from the heater. There was no provision for ventilation in an Anderson shelter. The 'all clear' sounded and we went back to the house. I remember hearing aircraft flying overhead and my mother assuring me they were British planes.

Some nights, we would stay with an aunt who lived on the outskirts of the city. My mother enjoyed being there and I loved being with my cousins. We were there on the night of the Coventry Blitz, 14 November 1940. That was the night the cathedral was bombed and virtually destroyed. Unfortunately, my uncle's shelter was flooded so when the siren sounded, my mother, aunt and two sisters went to a street shelter and my uncle took the rest of us to the shelter next door. I remember looking up into the sky, which was alight with searchlights and exploding shells and looking like a great firework display. I was the last to go down the steps into the shelter when a bomb dropped very close by. The blast lifted me off my feet and I fell down the ladder. It was a lucky escape, but I was not injured and only had some broken glass in my hair. Bombs were dropping and guns were firing and those silver barrage balloons were still there high up in the sky. There was so much noise and chaos, everyone was talking at once and I found it all very frightening.

We were worried about the rest of the family, but about three in the morning, a policeman came to our shelter to make sure we were unharmed and he told us that our the family was safe. He told us that unfortunately there had been a great deal of damage in the city.

When the 'all clear' sounded, we crept out of the shelter and found that a bomb had just missed my uncle's house. As we went inside we found my cousin's doll still sitting in the armchair covered in white dust but otherwise unharmed. My cousin just picked her up and cried with relief. The next day, we went home, wondering if our house had been damaged. Fortunately, we found it intact with just one broken window.

During the war, all windows were criss-crossed with brown sticky tape to stop glass from flying. We also had heavy blackout curtains so that not even a chink of light could be seen outside. It was thought that any light would help German bombers find their target.

My mother went to check on a friend who lived nearby. The house had been bombed, but fortunately all our friends were safe. It was an amazing sight, the roof and the outside walls of the house had disappeared. I could just see stairs and pictures askew on the walls. It looked like a dolls' house. From then on until this day whenever I see a dolls' house, I am reminded of that day.

Several hundred people lost their lives that night and the cathedral was destroyed by incendiary bombs. Gas and water pipes were badly damaged and there was fear of typhoid. The firemen were unable to get enough water to put the fires out so many buildings were damaged beyond repair.

When I was much older, I heard that the raids had lasted for thirteen hours and the flames could be seen 100 miles away, leaving the city vulnerable for the next raid.

Evacuation was not compulsory, but the government was very concerned for the welfare of children. It worked hard to persuade parents to allow their children to be evacuated away from the danger of bombing. My parents then decided I would have to go away and this time, there would be no return until the danger of bombing had ended. Our school was evacuated to Lighthorne near Leamington Spa. Lining up at the railway station, we all had luggage labels pinned to our coats showing our details, and we carried our gas masks over our shoulder. My mother and two sisters came to the school to wave me goodbye, they were upset and in tears but I just sat there in the coach determined not to let them see me crying. I knew that this time I could not persuade them to take me home with them. It was a very sad time for everyone.

When we arrived at Lighthorne, we went to the Malt house where we were told to sit quietly on the floor and to wait for a carer to come and collect us. We had no idea where we were going or who would look after us. After what seemed a long time, two ladies approached and asked my friend and I to go with them. One was the headmistress of the village school and the other was her sister. The schoolhouse was attached to the school and this was to be our home until the end of the war.

As we arrived, some children ran out of the school, some of them laughing. I just could not understand how they could feel happy. I thought I would never laugh again! However, we soon settled in and were treated kindly and I began to relax. The house we were living in had no running water and no flushing toilet. The toilet was at the end of the garden and although it was emptied every week, the smell was always terrible. Every morning we had to go to a well to fetch clean drinking water.

Our mothers came to visit us on Sunday afternoons and brought our sweet ration. I remember walking through the village to the bus to meet them. We were so excited. The next two years were peaceful. Our carers were very kind and allowed us a great deal of freedom. Our spare time was spent climbing trees, fishing and doing all the things a country girl would do, so very different from life in a city. There were too many children for us all to be taught in the little village school, so some classes were taught in stables belonging to the local squire. They had been thoroughly cleaned and all the walls were painted white. I remember learning how to do long division in that stable!

Clothes were on coupons, so I was lucky my mother was a clever dressmaker and hoarder of material. She made all our clothes for us so we were well dressed.

I went home for my sister's wedding to Bill, a bomber pilot; that was a very happy weekend for everyone. When I returned to Lighthorne, they both came to visit me. I was so pleased they did because I never saw my brother-in-law again. Soon after that, he was killed in a raid over Germany, along with my other sister's boyfriend who was the navigator on the same crew. The grief in our family was terrible. They had only been married for such a short time.

Eventually, all the evacuees returned to Coventry and I returned to my old school, I passed the scholarship and was given a place at Stoke Park Grammar School; I think I was lucky my education had not suffered.

When VE day and VJ day came, there was great rejoicing with street parties all over the city and I can remember the happiness and relief felt by everyone. It seemed strange to have street lights on again and not to have blackout curtains up at the windows.

It took some time for family life to get back to normal. Fathers, husbands and sons returned to their families but rationing continued and it took time for the shelves in shops to be refilled. It seemed a long time until sweet rationing ended.

Val is a widow now living in Wiltshire. She has three daughters and seven grandchildren. She trained as a nurse and married an RAF pilot.

Chapter 5

Hilde – 10 years old: Germany

I was 10 years old when war was declared and I remember it well. We lived in a small market town on Luneburg Heath, between Hanover and Hamburg. My parents sent my brother, sister and I to stay with my grandmother in the country.

My mother was nursing our younger sister who had diphtheria. She had heard of other children dying in hospital and felt it was safer to look after her at home. We were very fortunate that my father worked in the Post Office, which was considered to be a reserved occupation. That meant he did not have to go away to war.

For several weeks before war was declared, there had been a great deal of propaganda on the wireless and in the newspapers, causing considerable tension. I do not think anyone really expected England to declare war on Germany. We had seen in the cinema the strength of the German Army, with soldiers marching, tanks and large guns. We were also told that Germany had an impressive navy and air force.

We saw German soldiers marching into Austria where there seemed to be no resistance, just people cheering them. They went into Czechoslovakia and recovered the Sudetenland. We appeared to be so strong, surely no one would dare to oppose us! We were told that Germany was recovering land that rightfully belonged to Germany.

From 1939 onwards, all children from the age of 10 were expected to join the Hitler Youth. Everyone looked forward to joining and taking part in all the various activities and having a really good time. When I joined, I thought it was all wonderful. We went hiking, walking and camping in the forests and woods. In the evenings, after supper, we gathered round a campfire and sang traditional and patriotic songs. We were encouraged to take part in sport, as this helped develop a healthy body and mind. There were also many other activities we could take part in.

In addition to all this, we were given lectures on how well Germany was doing and all the good things that Herr Hitler had achieved, and wanted to achieve for the German people. We were told that Hitler was a wonderful man so I was surprised when my father did not agree with my ideas on the subject. He told me that I should never criticise anybody or anything outside the family and I must always be careful what I said as we never knew who we could trust. I always loved and trusted my father and felt very reassured when he told me he would always love his country come what may. The talks we were given at camps and meetings were very persuasive for young minds.

We were issued with ration books from early on in the war to ensure fair rations for everyone. However, towards the end of the war there was not enough food, even for rations. We were fortunate that we lived in the country and had a large garden where we grew vegetables and fruit. We also kept chickens, rabbits and a pig. People who lived in towns found it very difficult to find food and would eat anything they could find.

All German houses had cellars and we used ours to store vegetables in the winter and it was also used as an air raid shelter. When the sirens sounded we went into the cellar as quickly as possible but, as time passed by and we were not bombed, we often ignored the warnings.

Although there were regular bombings on Hanover, we still went for holidays to a hostel in a forest not far from the town. This was organised by the Hitler Youth. Early in the morning, we went for long runs and came back for a hearty breakfast. In the evenings, after a good supper, we spent time sitting around the campfire. For a very short time we could even forget there was a war on. There was a great feeling of camaraderie and we just enjoyed being in a beautiful, peaceful place. During this time, we collected acorns and beech nuts. The beech nuts were sent to a factory to be processed into beech oil for cooking, and the acorns were used as food for pigs.

For the first part of the war, our schooling continued as normal but, if a warning siren sounded, we were all sent home from school and went immediately into our cellars. Sometimes, we saw wave after wave of planes flying overhead. At first, we were frightened because we did not know if we were their target but, as time passed by, we realised that they were heading for Berlin and we felt very relieved that we were not the target. Sometimes, on a clear night we could see the very powerful searchlights over Hamburg and Hanover. We knew they were searching for the bombers.

Before the war, Hitler had done a great deal of good for Germany. He raised national morale, built autobahns and achieved many other good things, including getting people back to work. So, in the beginning, the people looked up to him. Unfortunately, he became greedy, and he hated the Jews.

There was a great deal of anti-Jewish propaganda around and people were told not to buy goods from Jewish shops, and not to mix with Jews. When my father bought a bed from a Jewish department store he had it delivered at night so that our neighbours would not see it being delivered. One night, a shop close to us, owned by a Jewish family, was burned down. Then, the department store was closed. People were shocked and gradually realised just how serious the situation was becoming. Any Jews living in our area suddenly disappeared and the Jewish children no longer came to school. We were never told where they went and no one dared to enquire. My parents told us to keep quiet and not to talk about anything outside the family. We never knew who we could trust.

Later in the war, refugees from East Germany and East Prussia arrived in our little town. They were trying to escape the fighting and the Russians. Most of them had left all their possessions behind. Every household was obliged to take them in and look after them. On one occasion, we had a family with five children staying with us. Our house was not big enough for this and my mother found it difficult looking after strangers, but there was no alternative. Even our school housed refugees and each day our class had to go to any available building in the town to have our lessons. We never knew where we would be from one day to the next!

We were lucky we had escaped most of the bombing. The only part of the town that was bombed was the railway station. A long train full of munitions going to the front was attacked by two British planes. They flew in very low, dropped their bombs and destroyed the train. There was a series of massive explosions, causing a great deal of damage to railway lines and the station. It was amazing that there were no civilian casualties, but we heard that many of the soldiers guarding the train were killed or injured.

In our family, my brother was called up and was being trained to go into the navy but, fortunately, the war ended before he went to sea. Sadly, my two young cousins went to war and one did not return. My younger cousin had given a false age and, despite his father going to see the recruiting officer and telling him that his son was still only 15, it was to no avail. He was told he was too late and nothing could be done to get his son back. We never heard of him or saw him again. Our whole family was devastated by this event.

We were encouraged to work after school and during the school holidays. For me, this involved staying on a farm twenty kilometres away, helping with the harvest and acting as an au pair to the large family. I had one day off a week and I would always cycle home in the late afternoon along a beautiful country road, flanked by large beech trees. One afternoon, I was cycling home for the weekend and was very surprised to see a long line of German soldiers walking towards me. They just looked ahead. No one waved or said anything. They looked dejected. There was no talking, just the sound of all the boots marching along. It was then that I realised – the army was retreating.

Two weeks later, when making the same journey, I passed an equally long line of British soldiers. They seemed much happier and called out and waved. I arrived home to find our house in darkness and my mother and father sitting in candlelight, as there was no electricity. My parents could not understand how I could cycle home when there was a strict curfew on. I had no idea there was a curfew and I had passed all the soldiers and nobody had stopped me.

We were still being fed propaganda on the radio and not being told the true situation but, by now, people were becoming sceptical and some were even questioning what was happening. One of our schoolmasters gathered the whole school together and told us that we were important members of the Hitler Youth and must be ready to fight and help the gallant soldiers of Germany. He was talking to some children as young as 11 and 12. Most adults just thought he was being ridiculous, but he really believed it was the right thing to do.

When the news about Belsen eventually became known, we were really shocked and surprised. We knew there were rehabilitation camps for politically unacceptable people and that Jewish people disappeared to another part of Germany, but we were not prepared for the horrors that became known when the camps were liberated. Nobody admitted to knowing about it. If they did know, they were too frightened to speak or to tell what they knew. Ordinary people felt very ashamed.

As the Allies made progress, life for Germans living in cities got worse. There was no electricity and no transport to bring food in from the countryside. The shops were empty and people were starving. The really good thing though, was that the bombing had stopped. When peace was signed, our area of Germany was all upside down. Shops, schools and civil offices had all closed down. At first the Americans occupied our zone but they were soon replaced by the British. Very gradually, life started to improve. I think America gave money and materials to help repair the damage that had been sustained. People who had committed terrible crimes against the local population were reported to the Allies and they were taken away for trial. It was a time for retribution.

Although the end of the war was a great relief, it was a very sad and tragic time for so many people. It took years for soldiers to return home. Many young men who went to fight on the Eastern front did not return and were never heard of again. Some returned injured, physically and mentally, and it took years for them to recover, if ever.

Hilde married an Englishman and still lives in the South of England with her sons.

Chapter 6

Hildegard – 11 years old: Germany

At the beginning of the war, I was living in Düsseldorf with my grandmother, who was a widow. My parents had separated and my three brothers were in care. We lived in a flat on the third floor. I think my grandmother found it difficult looking after a young girl, as there was always a shortage of money. Although she fed me and looked after me, she never showed any love or affection.

We could not afford a newspaper every day, but we did listen to the wireless, which was our main source of information. We were constantly reminded how strong and great Germany was. We were aware that Hitler had occupied Austria and had triumphantly recovered the Sudetenland for Germany. My grandmother was Polish by birth, but had married and lived in Germany for over thirty years. However, she always worried about her family and relatives in Poland.

Even before the war, we heard anti-Jewish propaganda and were told how the Jews were holding back the German economy. Anti-Jewish slogans appeared and young men in Hitler Youth or Nazi uniforms could be seen strutting around, trying to look important.

In Germany, when children were 10 years old they were expected to join the Hitler Youth, but I did not wish to. I was not an outdoor girl and did not fancy hiking in the woods or taking part in the other outdoor pursuits they were offering. We lived in a block of flats on the third floor and, in the flat beneath us, was a fervent Nazi family. They had a daughter of 16 who was a leader in the Hitler Youth and was very conscientious. When she realised I was over 10 and I had not joined, she reported me and I was visited by an official and told to join immediately or face the consequences.

Reluctantly, I joined the Hitler Youth and was given a uniform and went to the meetings every week. I think we were treated badly by the older leaders who were usually indoors in the warmth, chatting and flirting, while we younger children waited outside in the cold. Although they gave no thought to our welfare, most of the children did not seem to mind. They were all so keen on the organisation.

In each meeting, there was always a lecture, which was normally about how wonderful Hitler was. They said that he was a 'Father' to all his people and was doing great things for Germany. He promised a good life for everyone and said how important it was to have a healthy mind and body. He said that we children were the future of Germany and were superior to other races and we should always be proud that we were members of the 'Master Race'. He also said that the Jews plotted and worked against the state and one should keep away from them at school.

I did actually enjoy singing around campfires, where we learnt many traditional and patriotic songs and shared some very happy times.

On one great occasion, Hitler came to Düsseldorf. We all went to see him and to hear him speaking. It was an amazing sight. There were young people as far as the eye could see. All in uniform, giving the Nazi salute and chanting 'Sieg Heil, Sieg Heil'. Although I personally did not think he was charismatic, he created mass hysteria and it was easy to be carried away by it all. I was afraid to say anything, as someone might hear and report me and I could be sent away.

My grandmother had already been threatened because, instead of giving a Nazi salute to her neighbours one day, she greeted them by saying 'good morning' in German. They reminded her that she was Polish by birth and, if she stepped out of line, she would be transported to a concentration camp. Consequently, we lived in fear. Most of the inhabitants in the flats were friendly and pleasant, but we never knew who we could trust. People just disappeared and no one dared to ask any questions.

We had heard about concentration camps but we were informed that they were for resettlement, or places where people could be re-educated politically, especially those who plotted and worked against the state. This of course included the Jews.

As the war progressed, the bombing started and my schooling became disrupted. We were bombed by the British at night and the Americans by day. The cellar was the only safe place to be. One dreadful night our block was completely destroyed. Fortunately, we were in the cellar at the time. This was divided into little rooms which were, in normal times, used for storage. We were so lucky that the walls were thin because we had to break through five of them to escape. The planes had dropped incendiary bombs on the flats, so everything was destroyed by fire. We were all taken to a large bunker and given food and drink, and that is where we stayed the night.

The next morning we realised that we had lost our home and all our belongings, everything had gone. There were no buses or trams running, so we walked out of town to stay with an aunt. It took us over two hours, but at least we felt safer. We stayed there for over two years, with four of us living in a small one bedroom flat. Whenever there was a raid, we would go to a very large communal bunker. Amazingly, up to a thousand people sometimes took refuge there and we just had to find wooden benches to sit or sleep on. Here we found both soldiers and civilians and it was a very smelly, unpleasant place to be. We could always hear planes flying overhead. I could tell when they were British, as the sound of the engines was quite distinctive and different from the German planes.

My father went away to war on the first day in September 1939, but never returned. Eventually, we had the terrible news that he had died in 1945. He had been wounded and actually died of gangrene, just before Germany capitulated. If there had been medicines and antibiotics, he would probably have survived.

For nine months, the school I was attending was evacuated to Saxony in the countryside, far away from bombing. At last we lived in peace. Such a change from planes and bombs and damaged buildings.

Throughout the war we received food parcels from relatives in Poland. To me it always seemed strange that we were receiving food from an occupied country. During school holidays, I stayed with another aunt in the country. This was to give my grandmother a rest and it was also a good holiday for me.

Even before the war began there was anti-Jewish propaganda and we were told not to buy from Jewish shops and not to associate with Jewish people, as they were working against Germany. Opposite our flat there was a Jewish shoemaker, who worked there and lived above the shop. He had lived there for years and, before the war, he had a very successful business and had always been pleasant and helpful. One evening, we heard glass breaking and a great deal of shouting and noise. When we looked out of our window, we watched as things were being thrown out of his windows from the first floor. A piano, pictures, and two birdcages with birds in them, and then all their personal items came crashing to the ground. The little birds just flew away. The man and his family were then pushed and shoved into a lorry and taken away, never to be seen again. We could hear their shouts and cries. All their belongings were just left on the road. Eventually, people came and took anything they could salvage. Some even went into the flat and helped themselves to whatever they wanted.

Most people on the street just walked past as if nothing was happening. Everyone was afraid and no one wanted to be noticed. I can remember going into a shop for food and there, waiting to be served, was a Jewish man. People just pushed him out of the way and when it was his turn, the shopkeeper turned him away and told him there was no food left. This happened all the time. Jewish people were forced to wear the Star of David on their clothes, so it was easy to pick them out. Also, it was very difficult for them to get food. They were always asked to pay a great deal more money for everything.

My aunt worked for a Jewish couple before the war. The wife escaped to England, but her husband was sent to a concentration camp. He was a very rich man and managed to buy his way out and follow her. We heard later that he had died. I think the time he had spent in the concentration camp had taken its toll. We soon had no Jewish children at our school. Most Jews were rich and clever and they looked after each other. However, before long, there were no Jews left anywhere.

People were afraid of the Nazis and anyone in authority or uniform. The young men who looked so smart in their uniforms knew they were admired and they were very confident. Many girls thought they were wonderful and liked to be seen with them.

All through the war the wireless would report on how successful the raids on London had been and how well our brave soldiers were doing. No bad news was ever reported. At this time, although we were not aware of how close the British and American armies were, some people were beginning to wonder if Germany was losing the war.

One night I was asleep in the bunker when I was awakened by a very bright light in my eyes. It was an American soldier with a torch. He was telling us to go outside. At last, the Americans had arrived. Most people seemed glad, as it meant the war was nearly over. Also, they were very relieved that they were American and not Russian. We were really afraid of the Russians, we knew they raped women and young girls. The British and the Americans treated civilians well but, for some time, food was very scarce. People who lived in the country lived on vegetables and other home produced food but transport was virtually unobtainable, and it was not possible to take food into the towns, where people were starving. Electricity and drinking water were affected and only available at certain times of the day.

When the war ended there was so much to do. So many buildings and roads had to be rebuilt. Many lives had been turned upside down. Some fathers and husbands returned from POW camps, but many did not. Some never knew what had happened to their loved ones. By now, there were thousands of displaced persons, all looking for a new life in Britain, America or any country that would accept them.

It took time for people to realise that they could speak freely and not have the constant fear of someone knocking at their door in the early hours of the morning. It was difficult to accept that Germany had actually lost the war and that all the propaganda had been lies and just what the government wanted us to hear and to believe. It was hard to accept the horrors of the concentration camps. Until we actually saw the dreadful pictures, many people thought it was just American propaganda. We could not believe Germans could be responsible for such crimes. We finally realised that we were then the occupied country. When the British soldiers arrived and took control of the district they behaved well and life slowly improved, we began to realise that we could look ahead to a future.

Hildegard married an Englishman and now lives in the South of England with her husband and daughter.

Chapter 7

Colin – 4 years old: London, England

In September 1939 I was a 4-year-old. Although I did not understand what was happening. I just knew that my parents were very worried about something. I knew that when the siren ('Moaning Minnie') sounded, I had to make my way to the shelter in the garden. This was a foul smelling Anderson Shelter, already three inches deep in water. I found this a most unpleasant experience.

In 1940 bombs began to fall on London. One of these resulted in a tragedy that changed our lives forever. My father was the Station Master at Sloane Square underground station and this suffered a direct hit. He was one of the many people killed in this raid. This incident is well documented in *The Peoples War* by Angus Colder. I did not understand the consequences of this at the time, but I witnessed the devastating effect it had on my mother. I was aware that my father was no longer with us and our lives had changed forever.

My mother decided that my brother and I should stay at home rather than be evacuated with the rest of the school. After my father was killed, she was determined that we should stay together as a family. Many children in the area were evacuated and were sent to stay with strangers in the country. There were very few children of my age left behind.

When I was 5 years old I started school, and trundled along with my brother and the neighbour's children, each with lunchbox, satchel and the cardboard box, housing my gas mask, a horrible foul-smelling, claustrophobic item that I vowed never to wear.

The following is an extract from my observations recorded for posterity in my memoirs:

Observations on an Itinerant life

We had been told that the first thing that was going to happen, as soon as the war started, was that the Germans, whoever they were, were going to throw gas at us, so we had to have these gas masks with us at all times. The practice produced the spectacle of a school full of children frantically clamping these things over their faces as fast as they could, with the inevitable 'Smart Alecs' who could do it in three seconds flat. The ninnies could not manage at all, and there was every combination in between. Had there been a real gas attack, it's doubtful whether more than twenty per cent of us would have survived. In order to alert us to the possibility of instant annihilation, an Air Raid Siren would have sounded, a terrible whining contrivance that struck fear into all of who heard it. At the sound of this signal, the whole school would form a previously practised crocodile and then troop off quickly to the air raid shelter, clutching gas masks. When eventually the 'All Clear' sounded, they returned to the classroom again, arriving with at least three children missing and two extras we had not seen before.

Most had lost coats, gas masks and pencil cases. This procedure would be repeated at least three or four times a day and since this kind of pantomime went on for the first three years of my early schooling, it is hardly surprising that my preparation for future academic excellence was, to say the least, stunted! I can't remember actually learning anything there at all.

By 1941, bombs were a common occurrence and after a night of bombing and watching the sky over London turning red from the fires, we got up early and went out looking for shrapnel. This became a form of currency for us. If one retrieved a piece of shrapnel immediately after a raid and it was still warm it was more valuable. Shrapnel was jagged pieces of metal from anti-aircraft shells and bombs which came down everywhere. My brother was four years older than I was and he was in charge of me. This was a most exciting time for us. There was a certain freedom about life then and we moved around our neighbourhood without restriction.

In 1942, the Germans bombed an even wider area and, inevitably, our street was hit by a large land mine. This obliterated three houses and made a terrible mess of ours. These things floated down on parachutes and exploded before touching the ground, ensuring maximum damage. Fortunately, we were in the shelter at the time and were not hurt, but I do remember helping to dig out our neighbours' family. We found their entire large coal box had been blown down their garden, completely blocking their shelter door. Our house was too damaged to live in so, for a while, we went to Grandpa's in Ealing, which, oddly enough, was actually nearer the centre of the bombing. As children, we just seemed blasé about death and injuries and accepted that a neighbouring family, including two children had died the previous night.

In 1943 we came back to our newly repaired house. There was a scheme called the 'War Damage Reparation Scheme', which was responsible for ensuring that homes were repaired as soon as possible. Our home was just habitable and we were pleased to return. I think friends and relatives gave us some toys, furniture and other items to replace the ones we had lost. We also managed to buy some furniture and household items, although everything was difficult to find and there was little choice.

Coming back to our newly repaired house, we found the Americans had arrived and were billeted in houses just round the corner in another street. Things like nylons and chewing gum entered our lives. 'Got any gum chum?' was the local street cry. These American soldiers were very generous towards children and would give us chocolate, Hershey bars and chewing gum.

My mother left home early each morning and went to work in a munitions factory, which was really hard physical work. When she came home she cleaned the house and cooked a meal. After my brother and I had gone to bed she started her evening job. She had been a court dressmaker in her youth and was able to alter or make clothes for the local ladies. This brought in a much needed income. They brought material and clothes to be altered and remodelled and she made them up into new garments. She was very clever and was much in demand. Whenever a parachute came down in our vicinity my brother and I raced to retrieve it so that mother could use it to make clothes. Parachutes were made of high quality silk and floated down carrying flares, which helped the planes find their targets. After all this, she still found time to queue for food. She had no help and must have been exhausted at the end of each day, but I never heard her complain. It was a very difficult time for a young widow. However, she was always cheerful and just seemed to get on with life. Somehow she made the rations go round, but I can always remember feeling hungry. I enjoyed going to a nearby café with a penny and buying bread and dripping.

Sometimes barrage balloons came adrift and floated serenely over the roof tops at low level, trailing their cables causing damage to high chimneys. On days when there was no bombing or, even after a raid, we went out to play. Of course, the bombed buildings provided ideal areas for us to continue with our war games. Sometimes, we took 'possession' of a house and another gang tried to capture it from us. There was always plenty of ammunition lying around in the form of broken bricks, tiles, lumps of wood and metal bars. Sometimes, looking back, I wonder how nobody was killed or injured, just playing in that environment.

On the whole, we just got on with our lives. Our games on these danger-ous bomb sites resulted in bleeding arms and knees, which were just part of daily life. If a policeman appeared, we just scattered until the coast was clear. We were all afraid of policemen and authority and tried to avoid them at all times. I joined the Boys Brigade and really enjoyed marching to church on Sundays with drums, bugles and flags flying, making as much noise as possible! We felt proud wearing a uniform and actually believed we were helping the war effort.

In 1944, having failed to break the country's spirit with normal warfare, Hitler resorted to his '*Vergeltungswaffen*', or revenge weapons, namely the V1 and V2. The former, was the 'flying bomb' or 'doodlebug', as it was nicknamed. When we heard one coming and its engine suddenly stopped, it would dive down and explode causing a great deal of damage. It was such a relief when one had passed over.

The V2 was a different story; this was the world's first ICBM. (intercon-tinental ballistic missile). We could not see or hear it coming, there was no warning and people realised they were unable to protect themselves. It was a frightening situation and one that was out of our control. One did land near us and the devastation was horrific. A whole line of houses just disappeared and the people inside were all killed.

In 1945 the German surrender brought everyone out onto the streets of London. At last the war was over. 'VE Day' was declared. Street parties and celebrations followed, which seemed to last for ages. My mother took us into the centre of London and we all stood on Westminster Bridge among a crowd of thousands. It was rumoured that Winston Churchill was going to make an appearance. People were singing, dancing and climbing every van-tage point, trying to catch a glimpse of him. I was so frightened in case I got lost. My mother was crying with relief and emotion, she just said she wished my father could have been there. At last, the war was over, it was certainly a happy time for many people, but a very sad time for others.

Looking back on all that had happened, the war certainly took its toll of London. The docks and buildings everywhere were badly damaged. Work started on the reconstruction of the city, but it took a long time to get back to normal. Women waited for their husbands, and children for fathers to return. Soldiers and PoWs came home and demobilisation from the three services started. However, so many did not return and some came back injured physically and mentally.

Colin lives in the South of England. He is an artist with two sons.

Chapter 8

Angie – 9 years old: London, England

Although I was 9 years old, I was not really aware of war approaching. I heard my parents talking about it to my brothers but, to me, it did not seem very important. At that time, I was attending a little school not far from home. I saw air raid shelters being built and, from time to time, barrage balloons being raised and lowered. I did not like these at all and thought they looked rather threatening.

One morning, my brother came to me and said: 'War has been declared!' He had just heard this on the wireless.

Within a few nights, searchlights could be seen sweeping the sky looking for any German aircraft but fortunately these did not arrive for some time. Occasionally, we saw British aircraft practising for future battles. We lived in Virginia Water, on the outskirts of London, which turned out to be on the flight path for bombers heading for the city.

My mother started making black curtains for our windows. This was obligatory and they had to completely cover every window in the house. We also had to stick brown tape over our windowpanes, in order to prevent any flying glass caused by bomb blasts coming into the rooms and injuring us.

Gas masks were issued in brown cardboard boxes. Younger children were given a gas mask bag. The little boy next door was given one of these and hated going inside and always cried when there was a practice. We were then issued with sandbags and my father and brother filled them and piled them carefully outside against our windows and walls. That was when I realised we were in a dangerous situation. Before long, we could hear the bombers droning as they flew overhead. By now the sirens sounded every night. It was then that my parents decided that it would be safer to sleep downstairs. We could never rely on a peaceful night and always had to be prepared for the warning sound of the sirens. Sometimes we just went into the cupboard under the stairs, but mostly we went to the air raid shelter at the bottom of the garden. This was quite horrid and it often flooded, it always seemed to be cold, dark and miserable. I really hated it. We eventually had a paraffin heater and candles, which made it slightly better.

Most nights the bombers flew over our house heading towards the centre of London, fortunately we were not the target. Sometimes, when returning to Germany, enemy aircraft would drop any bombs left on board at random. This meant one could never relax until the all clear had sounded.

At this time, the water in the lake at Virginia Water was drained. We were told that this was necessary because the water in the lake shone in the moonlight, giving enemy bombers a wonderful landmark. It was refilled as soon as hostilities ended. The Thames of course, was the other major landmark that helped to guide the German bombers to London.

My father joined the army, in the Intelligence Corps, and spent most of the war in Yorkshire and Oxford. We were so lucky that we managed to see him in the school holidays. Then, we would go up to Yorkshire and would stay in a friend's house. It was wonderful being there, as we could sleep in proper beds with sheets and blankets and roam around the countryside in relative safety.

My brother and I were sent to boarding school when I was 10. It was not far from home and I always worried about my mother's safety. Every night after supper, our teachers took us down to the temporary dormitories in the cellar. I can still remember seeing them standing there in their dressing gowns, wearing tin hats and slippers! We wondered why they had tin hats but we did not! The school thought it would be safer for us to be there all night, rather than to sleep in the main dormitories and be evacuated when there was an air raid.

During term time the school kept our ration books. I can remember after lunch each day, a tray of sweets came round and we were allowed to take just one. We had an American girl at the school who received large parcels of sweets from America. It seemed unfair to me that she was only allowed to take one, but she just wanted to be the same as everyone else.

I know I always felt hungry and I asked my mother to write to the school asking for more food for me but unfortunately, I did not get any more. I think growing girls always feel hungry. We were always active and busy.

One difficulty my mother had was that, even though there was a war on, the school still had a strict uniform code. Everyone had an allowance of clothing coupons, but we were expected to have so many pairs of pants, socks, and other clothes that most of my clothing coupons were used when purchasing my uniform. It must have been difficult for my mother to manage. I remember I had large hems on clothes and everything was bought with the idea that I would eventually grow into them.

Later in the war we had flying bombs, known as 'Doodle Bugs', to contend with. One of them landed close by, in the woods just outside the grounds of the school. All the school windows were blown in and there was glass everywhere. Fortunately no one was hurt. We were sent home for an extra week's holiday while the glass was put back in the windows. As the flying bombs flew over we always prayed that their engines would keep going. Once their engines stopped, they would fall vertically down and cause enormous destruction. I will never forget that unique engine noise.

After the London Blitz, so many people in London had lost their homes and my mother was obliged to take in some evacuees. This was a family that had been bombed out of their home in the East End. When the husband returned from Dunkirk, he found their home had been destroyed and the family had nowhere to go. It was not an ideal situation, but everyone accepted it. My mother always said there was a war on and everyone had to make sacrifices.

Eventually in 1945 the war ended and my father left the army and returned to civilian life. The shops seemed empty and rationing continued, but we were back as a family again and my parents seemed relaxed and happy. I think I was very lucky to have lived where I did, as there was very little damage to our neighbourhood. I was fortunate not to have had disrupted education. We were also very lucky not to have any member of the family killed or injured.

The following are three extracts from letters Angie sent home from her school.

23 January (no year)
'On Friday night we had 3 raids. There was a lot of gunfire. There is one new girl this term.'

19 March (no year)
'On Wednesday we went down to the cellar. It was horrible because aeroplanes were so near and I thought they were going to dive bomb us. On Friday we went down again but nothing much happened. Yesterday we went for a walk.'

20 March (no year)
'Mummy sent me two oranges this week. We had another raid the other night with a lot of gunfire and a bomb landed on the London line, everybody had to go round on the Weybridge line. I will be seeing you soon ....'

All of these letters are very matter of fact, but it must have been a frightening time for a young girl.

Angela married a naval officer and had three children. She is now a widow and lives in Hampshire.

Chapter 9

Eric – 12 years old: Wimborne, England

I was born in Wimborne, Dorset at the end of 1927. When war was declared I was at Wimborne Council School.

My first inkling of impending war was from the wireless and from my parents talking. Then, one day in September, I was sent to buy *The Daily Herald*, and as I left the shop I looked at the front page. The headlines were huge: 'War Declared'.

For a little time nothing much happened. Then there was talk of forming the Local Defence Volunteers. These were mature men who formed groups with any sort of weapon available, hunting rifles, shotguns, old pistols even wooden poles!

As time passed, this became more organised and it became the Home Guard. Eventually the ARP was formed, this included local councillors, retired men and old soldiers.

Men from the ARP came to our school and asked for volunteer messengers, I thought this would be exciting so I volunteered. We used our bicycles to carry these messages from one ARP post to another. This was necessary because in those days very few people had phones in their houses and had to rely on public phone boxes. I looked forward to this thrilling duty and felt very important. Occasionally, the siren sounded while I was delivering a message and then it really was exciting.

One day we arrived at school to find deep trenches being dug in our playing fields, these were in a zigzag pattern very similar to those used in the First World War. When there was an air raid we were all ushered out of school into these trenches, supervised by the teachers. I cannot imagine how this could have given us any protection in an air raid. However, every school had to have some form of shelter for the pupils.

We didn't know what to expect, I think we were very apprehensive and afraid. Above us in the skies we could see the fighter aircraft making crazy patterns across the blue sky, shooting at enemy air craft and, very occasionally, a plane would fall to earth surrounded by flames. My brothers and I spent endless time watching these 'dog fights'.

We were issued with gas masks and instructed in their use, they came in strong cardboard boxes with a cord attached, to wear around the neck or over the shoulder. It had to be carried at all times.

As the war progressed we had evacuees sent to our area, an obvious choice as we lived in the country, which was considered a safer place to be. Most of the children came from Southampton, which of course was a prime target as it had large docks and industry, which included the Supermarine Spitfire works.

Apart from finding billets for this large influx of children, they posed a problem for the education authorities in the area. As a result, the local Methodist church hall was used for some lessons. A new experience, but a good one and we all mixed well. Their accommodation varied enormously and keeping in touch with absent parents was not always easy. With constant air raids at home, children were worried about their parents and I think most of them were homesick too.

Air raid shelters were built everywhere. Some were built of brick and concrete, others were Anderson shelters made of corrugated iron, similar to mini Nissan huts. We built our own with the help of friends by excavating a large ditch and covering it over with soil and turf. I was not very happy when I had to sleep there; it was always so cold and miserable inside.

Before long we were issued with ration books. Everyone was allocated coupons for a certain amount of basic food, meat, butter, margarine, cheese, sugar, and sweets to name some. Petrol was also rationed, but only people such as doctors and key personnel were entitled to drive cars. We all used our bicycles to get around. We were aware that some goods were available on the 'Black Market', but that was a risky business as one could be sent to jail if caught. We lived in the country and my uncle often supplied us with rabbits, which supplemented the meat ration. We also grew vegetables and fruit, which helped my mother a great deal for her cooking and planning meals for us.

We lived close to the Somerset and Dorset railway line and frequently saw the freight and troop trains passing by. One night, I was awakened by a very loud bang followed by four more, the house shook and a window pane cracked, bombs had fallen about half a mile away, leaving deep craters in the landscape.

We heard that a train had been signalled to stop in a deep cutting. Unfortunately, the fireman opened the furnace door and this sent a bright shaft of light skywards. The German pilot flying above spotted this, he could see the outline of the train so dropped his bombs. Fortunately, he missed the train and the houses in the nearby village. We soon realised we were on the flight path of the German bombers.

When I was 16 I joined the Army Cadet Force. I was interested in Morse Code, so became a signaller, we also had to learn semaphore. Although we didn't realise it at the time, we were being trained for the army. I really enjoyed playing in the Cadet Bugle Band. Every Sunday, we would march through the town making a great deal of noise and feeling very smart in our uniforms.

One night we saw a large orange glow in the sky, this persisted for several nights and we heard that Southampton Docks and some meat stores, had been set on fire. These fires were so fierce they could not be extinguished easily.

People were very anxious about incendiary bombs, which fell in great numbers, setting fire to any buildings they landed upon. One day we heard that a German plane had been shot down about a mile away. When my friend and I arrived, the police were there and they allowed us to look for souvenirs. I found a piece of an aircraft with a swastika on it and my friend found the handle of a broken revolver. We later discovered that the crew had parachuted out and were safe; they had been taken prisoner.

At last, the Americans arrived in the village where they requisitioned several large houses. Before long the area became saturated with troops, both American and British, with their tanks. These large vehicles would drive through the village, before heading for the Purbeck hills where tank driving was taught and manoeuvres took place. We later found out that this was the beginning of the preparations for D Day. We became very aware of aircraft in the skies and we knew something was about to happen.

I left school and started work in an engineering works in Poole. I used to cycle there each day and on the way, I passed a factory where machine guns were made. The Americans brought in vehicles to waterproof the engines and to store them. We thought it a very strange thing to do. We later realised that these were in preparation for the forthcoming invasion into Normandy, France.

We heard on the wireless news when the assault had begun. The Pathe News, at the cinema, gave good coverage of the advance into Germany and other news of events as they occurred in Europe. As the allied troops moved forward and the concentration camps were being liberated, we saw terrible pictures of skeletal prisoners and piles of dead bodies. Nobody believed that the Germans could have behaved in such an inhuman way. It was very shocking, as we had not realised this was happening.

On VE day, my friend and I cycled to Poole Park, there was a fantastic atmosphere with bands playing, people singing and dancing, and everyone thoroughly enjoying themselves. All the pubs were doing a roaring trade, thankfully no one asked how old we were! We had such fun.

Although the war was over, I received call up papers in early 1946 and I spent two and a half years in the army, where I spent most of the time in the Middle East and North Africa.

Eric lives in Hampshire with his wife, sadly his only son died a few years ago. He has two grandchildren. For many years he taught welding to students.

Chapter 10

Jon – 4 years old: The Netherlands

When war was declared in 1939, Jon lived in Rotterdam, in an apartment with his family.

The Netherlands was a neutral country in the First World War and everyone assumed the same would happen in the second. In 1940 the Germans threatened the Dutch Government that, if they did not surrender, they would bomb the main cities of Amsterdam, Rotterdam and The Hague. One morning, Jon saw a large number of planes flying over. Everyone who saw them thought they were going to bomb England but, once over the sea, they turned round and came back and bombed Rotterdam. Before long, the city was swamped with German soldiers, tanks and troop carriers. The people of the Netherlands were ill-prepared for the next five years of occupation.

It was a bad time for everyone and no one knew what would happen next. People did not know if they would be searched for contraband or if their bicycles would be taken away.

What follows is Jon's account of his war:

It all started with the Germans dropping bombs on Rotterdam airport on 10 May 1940. This raid was followed by a massive German advance towards the bridges, south of the Rhine. The Dutch Royal Marines held out until 14 May. They had their headquarters in Rotterdam, but they were no match for the might of the German Army, with modern tanks, guns and a very powerful air force and navy.

Even though an end to the fighting had been negotiated, this was ignored and some hundred German aircraft dropped incendiary bombs on the centre of Rotterdam and the port area. Within twenty minutes, they levelled one square mile in the centre. Over 25,000 homes, 775 warehouses, twenty-four churches, 2,320 stores and sixty-two schools were burnt down, making some 85,000 people homeless. The devastation was incredible and it took two years to clear the rubble.

The canals and smaller harbours in Rotterdam were all filled with the rubble. For many years, the trams could not run because there was no electricity and the tracks had been destroyed. Most of the time, people used bicycles or walked to work or school.

My mother's younger sister was in hospital in Rotterdam West, but we lived in Hillegersberg, one of the North Eastern suburbs. The only way we could get there was on foot. We had to pass regular checkpoints, where my mother's bag and even my clothes were checked for contraband.

One morning on our way to school, we witnessed a terrible event. German soldiers gathered a group of men together, put them against a wall and shot them as a reprisal for the events the night before. This did not happen just once, it happened at regular intervals. It always seemed to be early in the morning when we were going to school. The Germans took reprisals every time the resistance acted against them.

Wirelesses were not permitted, so my father built his own. If anyone was caught in possession of a wireless the punishment was severe. One might be sent to a concentration camp or shot. He made a housing for this in the shape of a Bible and placed it among the other books on our bookshelf so that if any German came into the house, they would not see it. Whenever this happened, my mother took me out of the way as she was worried I might say something. The Germans came regularly to check that there were no boys living in the house who were old enough to be sent to work in Germany. Some of the officers were courteous, but others were clearly Nazi and I found them frightening.

Every evening my father listened to the BBC from London. This, of course, was an activity that was banned by the Germans. For the wireless to work, my father turned a wheel with a dynamo attached.

He worked for one of the ministries and I discovered much later that he also acted as a courier for the Resistance. He was a very brave man in a very dangerous job.

Our primary school was taken over and occupied by German troops. When this happened, we had to walk past it every day to have our lessons in the Grammar School. With so many children, the building was severely overcrowded, but there was no alternative. We felt we were lucky to be able to go to school so our education could continue and was not too disrupted.

Food was getting more expensive, so any spare land was dug up and turned into allotments.

In 1942, the Germans started to pick up men without jobs in the age group of 18 to 35. They transported them to work in Germany. That year, they took away 19,000 men. Unfortunately, my eldest brother was picked up and did not return until late 1946, a year after the war had ended.

In 1943 there was a General Strike. As a punishment the Germans dealt with this by picking up many people. The lucky ones were sent to labour camps in Germany, but the leaders were all shot. Unfortunately we witnessed this too, on our way to school. By now the Resistance was becoming more organised and increasingly daring. Once, they shot the German head of police, another time they raided the local jail and freed some Resistance workers. They performed many dangerous deeds and worked hard to disrupt the enemy. They also supplied the British with valuable information about troop movements. Later in the war they informed them about the V1 and V2 launching sites that were situated nearby.

Gradually, items like textiles and shoes became scarce and prices went up and up. I had wooden clogs to wear, these had a layer of straw inside them, as they were one size too large. If I had to run, I took my clogs off so that I could run faster. Eventually, the soles wore out and my father used old inner tyres to remake them. Band Iron held the clogs together once they started to split.

Our bikes, by then, had lost their tyres and the wooden replacements had gone as well. We just used the bare rims and did our best to cycle. At this time the Germans had begun to hoard machinery, cars and bicycles, which they subsequently sent on to Germany. One did not dare leave a bicycle or any other valuable equipment unattended.

The Dutch always kept very good records. Everything was recorded and registered. Hence, when the Germans wanted to pick up the Jews, all they had to do was to go through the card index at the local Town Hall. Thus, they got names and addresses and simply went to their homes to round them up. At the beginning of the war, there were 13,000 Jews in Rotterdam. By 1945 only 700 were left.

About a mile and a half behind our house there were launching pads for the V1 and V2 Weapons. This was the flying bomb and the V2 rocket. They flew over our house, heading straight for England. Sometimes you heard the engines stop, due to a malfunction. Whenever this happened, we ran like mad and got downstairs to our emergency shelter in the cellar.

At the beginning of the war, my father decided to make up some emergency packs of food. He put tea, coffee, crackers, and dried milk in plastic cartons and left them in the cellar, just in case we were marooned down there. This never happened but it wasn't long before we had used up all these precious supplies and there was nothing left. To begin with we replaced any food consumed, but before long there were no supplies left at all.

The Razzias started up again. This time, men and boys between the ages of 16 and 45 were picked up and sent away. The German soldiers just waited outside cinemas and football stadiums and when the men came out, they arrested them. In two days, 11 and 12 November, 40,000 men were sent away to work in factories in Germany.

Winter came, the rivers froze, and consequently, no boats with food or coal could reach us. Electricity became scarce and then not available at all to households. Medications were in short supply too. However, we became inventive, making candles just to get a little light. To get more light my father erected a windmill linked to a bicycle dynamo and this actually lit a bicycle bulb.

In September 1944, the Allies were getting closer and the Germans introduced a curfew. Everyone had to be indoors between 8pm and 4am. The advance of the Allies was slowed down by fierce fighting and they were held up between the two rivers which isolated Rotterdam from the South of the Netherlands. The Germans reinforced their fortifications in the town, with guards on all the bridges. The main section of Hillegersberg was between the lakes, so it was easy for the Germans to check everything and everybody. I was regularly checked and searched on my way to and from school and had to answer all sorts of questions.

Food was still rationed and went from 1,350 calories a day to 300 calories a day in January. We ate potato peelings, sugar beet and even tulip bulbs. A soup that was grey and thin was termed 'grey field mouse soup'. This was cooked in field kitchens and made from peelings and anything else that was available, but not field mice! My father was in charge of one of these kitchens, which did its best to feed the community. Some of the local children were extremely thin, malnourished and very poorly. Some died from malnutrition.

We had a little round stove in one of the rooms, which burnt everything. Rapidly, all wood in the area disappeared. No fencing, trees or anything that could be burnt remained. We even sifted the coal ash paths for pieces of coal.

Despite all the hunger we felt there was one incident that made us all laugh. My father had managed to cook some sugar beet in order to make syrup. When ready, he put a jar on the stove and poured the syrup in. Hot into cold. The jar cracked and all the precious syrup was lost. I still hear my father reciting the alphabet in swear words!

In March 1945, the people in Rotterdam were starving and the Germans reached an agreement with the Allies. It was agreed that they could drop food by air for the civilian population. They had to fly along an agreed safe corridor at a low level between 150ft and 450ft. The first food to come was Swedish white bread and pure butter. This was a real treat. Then, in late March, lots of aeroplanes flew over and, behind our house, the sky was full of parachutes with crates of food. Some crates of food were dropped without parachutes. We ran to the field as quickly as we could before we were chased away by German soldiers. I managed to snatch a bar of chocolate, which I ate straight away. I was so sick; my stomach could not cope with such rich food. We heard later that the Germans had orders not to touch any of the food, they just stood by so that the Dutch authorities could organise a fair distribution. This saved many lives and raised morale as we knew the end of the war was nearly there.

On 5 May 1945, some months after the south of the Netherlands had been liberated, the Canadians arrived in Rotterdam. What a sight! There were flags everywhere. We had rides in their jeeps, we sat on their tanks and everyone had an amazing party!

There were repercussions for some within the community however. Women who had befriended German soldiers and had collaborated had their hair shaven. Men who had collaborated with the Germans and acted against their own people were escorted to jail without exception or excuse.

More civilians died of starvation during the war than for any other reason. This is why, even now, I cannot stand seeing children in restaurants ordering food and not eating it. To me that is a crime.

Jon is married and lives in the south of England

Chapter 11

Greta – 7 years old: Elverum, Norway

I was 7 years old when war was declared. For Norwegians, it started on 9 April 1940. Before this, Poland and Czechoslovakia had been invaded and occupied by the Germans. We were aware of what was happening in the rest of Europe as we listened to the wireless every day and also read the newspapers, which gave us the latest news. We all listened to the BBC so we were kept well informed. We were worried that we also could be invaded. Although we had an army, an air force, a small navy and a large merchant navy, we knew we were no match for the might of the German Army, which just seemed to sweep through the rest of Europe.

It was reported on the wireless that several German ships were sailing up the Oslo fjord. These looked as if they were the first part of the occupying army. Fortunately, we managed to sink the flagship which was called the *Blucher* and all on board were drowned. This was carrying 1,500 soldiers and SS men. They were coming to arrest our king and to occupy our country. When the ship was sunk one of the main concerns was that the oil on board would come to the surface and damage marine life, a rich source of our food.

The sinking of the flagship and the damaging of several other ships gave the Norwegian Royal family a little valuable time to escape. The rest of the invading army landed some fifty miles from Oslo and then made its way to the capital. German parachutists also landed at Oslo and Stavanger airports. At the same time, Germans landed at Narvic, Stavanger and Trondheim. Much to the disgust of the Norwegian people, German troops entered Oslo playing a military band. We were not prepared for this.

One night at about midnight, before all this happened, we were awakened by loud banging on our front door. My father was an officer in the King's Guard and a young soldier had come to tell him that he must report immediately to his unit in Elverum. This was where the royal family and the government had retreated to. He was informed that war was about to be declared. We did not know what was happening and my three sisters and I were very frightened. Unfortunately in those days, houses did not have telephones. He put on his best uniform and belt at once and then he and my mother left the house. Before leaving, she told us to stay in bed, to go to sleep and she would be back in the morning. However, she only went a little way with him and then returned. We were very worried, because we just did not know what was going to happen and we thought we may never see our father again.

In Elverum, the government loyal to the king advised that, to avoid being captured by the Germans, the royal family must leave immediately and escape to England. The British royal family had offered them a safe haven. As a member of the King's Troop, my father was directly involved in the evacuation of the royal family. As part of the rear guard action, he was given orders to destroy bridges and to blow up the railway lines with dynamite. This was an attempt to slow down the German Army and their Quisling collaborators. During their journey to the coast, the royal party was hidden by local farmers who, although it was very dangerous, were only too happy to help and protect their king. They then boarded HMS *Devonshire* for their voyage to England, where they stayed for the duration of the war.

My father and colleagues were ordered to find their way home after they had completed their work. On no account should they allow themselves to be captured by the Germans, or by German sympathisers, and taken prisoner. For helping the king to escape they would almost certainly have been shot.

A man called Knut Vikenes gave my father shelter for about a week. He decided it was necessary to burn his uniform and any other evidence which could be used to identify him as a soldier. Then Knut gave him some farm clothes to wear. He kept 'an agenda' (diary) which gave the details and information about their undercover work and he asked Knut to hide it and keep it safe for him until he returned after the war. He then left the farm and made his way home over the mountains, arriving back some twenty days later. It had been a very hazardous journey. He had managed to find shelter in the mountain huts normally used by skiers and farmers. We were so happy and relieved to have him back.

This diary is now in the museum in Elverum. It is an amazing account of what happened until the king made his escape and it includes drawings of the bridges and the railway lines they had blown up. It was signed by my father and it remained in the loft of Knut's barn for over sixty years. It was finally discovered in 2002, when the barn was demolished. Everyone had forgotten it existed. Our family knew nothing about it.

After the war started, we were advised to leave home and go to the country for safety. We packed a few belongings and left. For a few days, we stayed anywhere we could but then my mother decided we would be better back at home, so we walked back. It was so good to be back in our own house, in our own beds with our toys and belongings.

I started school in the August of that year. On the whole, the school was not affected by the Germans. However, on 17 May 1941, the day Norway always celebrates its constitution, the teachers told us that we were going into the woods for an outing. All national celebrations were banned by the Germans and we were not allowed to fly National Flags. However, when we arrived at a clearing in the woods, our teachers told us to sit in a large circle. They stuck flags in the ground, we sang National songs and our Anthem. We had a picnic, played games and had a really exciting day. We were told that this episode was to be our secret and we could only talk about it in our homes not outside, as someone might report this event to the Germans and we could all be in serious trouble.

The ordinary German soldiers did not bother us but we were very frightened of the SS in their black uniforms, and there was strict discipline if a child misbehaved. One young boy we knew was taken by the SS and beaten so badly that they nearly killed him. We just tried not to be noticed. We never knew how he had displeased the SS, but we knew that if we disobeyed any order, we would be harshly dealt with. My grandfather, who was a dairy farmer, was forced to give half of his milk every day to the Germans. All farmers had to do this. The Germans went round the countryside collecting food to feed the soldiers and to send any surplus back to Germany.

We were lucky that we had grandparents and other relatives with farms. We grew our own vegetables and fruit and had chickens, rabbits and a pig, so we were never really hungry.

As time went by, food became scarce and strict rationing came in very quickly. There was very little food of any kind in the shops and certainly no luxuries. People who lived in towns and cities were almost starving.

My mother was not short of money but she did find some food difficult to obtain. For a time she worked at a farm, washing floors to obtain three loaves of bread each day, freshly baked by the farmer's wife. We needed milk and I went to a farm run by Nazi sympathisers. Our neighbours were not happy but my mother just said her children needed milk. We knew of one lady who, when returning from a farm with her son, was stopped by a German soldier and questioned. When he saw that she had milk in a jug he just poured it on to the ground. They could do nothing about it and returned home empty handed.

My father managed to barter and obtained a crate of sardines in oil. He also managed to get a sack of wheat from a farm. In the middle of the night, he put it on a cart and took it to the miller who ground it into flour for him. This enabled my mother to bake bread and a form of biscuit, for a little while. White bread was such a treat.

Punishment for disobeying rules was death or being sent away to a labour camp.

Soon the Germans occupied the whole country. If people resisted or acted against them, they were shot. At one time, there were 300,000 German soldiers in Norway and they had to be fed by food grown from Norway.

They took over a factory making potato flour. Then, they told my father that he must take over the running of the factory and start making wooden cupboards and furniture for the Germans. They told him that if he refused, he would be sent to a camp in the North or to Germany. They had camps for anyone who did not do as they were told. My father did not want to do this, but he had to think of his family and of the workers who relied on him. Before the war he was a builder and carpenter by trade and had built up a small business.

Our prime minister was Vidrun Quisling, a supporter of the Nazi regime. He tried to impose Nazi ideals on Norwegian society but, when the people saw how he sent over 700 Jews to Auschwitz and threatened martial law and internment, most of his support was lost.

However, several farmers nearby were behind him. We could not talk freely in case we were reported. One Saturday, my father said 'Greta get your bicycle. I want you to put this paper inside your stocking and take it to your Aunt Margit. You must not stop or talk to anyone'. I cycled there and saw Margit. She was expecting the leaflet and took it from my stocking immediately. All over the country leaflets were secretly being printed, copied and circulated to people so that they would not believe the German propaganda. These leaflets also mentioned any action that had been carried out by the Resistance.

Immediately after a raid or some other action, the Germans would take reprisals. One never knew if there would be a knock on the door and someone would be taken away.

We were told that we should only talk to Germans if we had to. If we were travelling on a bus or train, we should not sit next to them. When the Germans realised this was happening they made it illegal to stand on a bus or train if a seat next to a German was available. Students and people all over Norway wore a paper clip in their lapel to show solidarity with the resistance. I do not think the Germans knew this was happening.

All through the war our family and friends had faith that Germany would be defeated in the end. The BBC helped to keep this alive. Crown Prince

Olav broadcast messages of encouragement to his people from time to time. His broadcasts certainly gave people hope for the future. Even though it was very dangerous to listen to these broadcasts, people still had sets hidden in safe places. Everyone knew that if they were caught and a wireless was discovered, they would either be shot or sent to a concentration camp in Germany.

Some people went into the mountains to grow tobacco some even grew it in their lofts. So many things were banned and, if caught, the guilty person would be dealt with severely.

Our area was not bombed by the Germans, but the RAF attacked Nazi headquarters in Oslo and also German ships in the harbours. These raids continued for about two years. A large number of young men had succeeded in getting to England to fight against the Germans. All over Norway young men and women joined the Resistance and regularly committed acts of sabotage. They were very brave and worked hard to disrupt the Germans. My father had several cousins who were involved. Three escaped to Sweden though one was shot trying to escape.

One thing the Germans miscalculated, was the length of our border with Sweden. This made it impossible for them to stop resistance workers or refugees crossing into safety .The Swedish people were very good to their Norwegian cousins and regularly sent food parcels which were so welcome. These came through the International Red Cross. I can remember opening these parcels to find out what we had been given. My mother was always delighted with whatever we received.

At the end of the war we heard that the Germans had burnt forests, towns and villages in the North. This 'scorched earth' policy was designed to hinder a possible attack on the Germans by the Russians. They were very afraid of the Russians and what they might do.

When the war ended in 1945, the royal family returned to Norway. It was a truly amazing time. When they arrived by ship, enormous crowds came to see their beloved king and queen. My family could not go but we heard all about it on the wireless and saw it at the cinema. What a sight after five years of war! It was wonderful to see Norwegian flags flying everywhere and no more German flags.

Life was not so easy for all at this time. Girls who had befriended Germans had their heads shaved and followers of Quisling were arrested and some were even shot. Vidrun Quisling was shot as a traitor. After the war, German PoWs were used to clear minefields. This was supervised by British and Norwegian troops.

It took many years for the people of Norway to get back to normal life. Even to this day, the king sends a very large Christmas tree, on behalf of the Norwegian people, as a thank you for supporting Norway during those terrible years. This stands proudly in Trafalgar Square over the Christmas period each year.

Greta now lives in Spain and regularly visits her family in Norway. She is a widow. She worked for several years on a newspaper.

Chapter 12

Three short accounts ...

This chapter contains memories from three different individuals.

Paula – 12 years old: Paris, France

When war was declared I was living in Paris with my mother, father and two sisters. Although we heard all about a possible war, nobody really believed it would happen so quickly. I think they thought if a war happened, it would be similar to the First World War. The Maginot line had been built to stop an advancing army. People talked about the Maginot line as our main line of defence, but I do not think they could believe it would hold up a modern German army. There were still so many people in France who remembered the horrors of the First World War.

My father immediately joined the army and left home and my mother went back to nursing. We soon realised that the Germans were heading for Paris and my parents thought it would be far too dangerous for us to be there.

It was then decided that my sisters and I should go to relatives in Carcassonne, in the south of France. Before the Germans entered Paris however, my mother joined us in Carcassonne. An aunt who lived in Algiers came over to persuade us all to leave France and go back with her. This was where we always went for our summer holidays and she felt we would all be much safer there with her and my grandparents. After a great deal of discussion, my mother agreed that we should all go for an extended summer holiday, nobody thought the war would continue for five years. Once there, we realised that there were no more ships going back to France, we were trapped.

We were very lucky we had family beyond France who were happy to have us with them and to support us until the end of the war. However, before long things became difficult. We were very poor, as no money could be sent from France and we always seemed to be growing out of clothes and shoes. We could only occasionally buy cheap shoes and material from the market. My mother had a local dressmaker who made our clothes, she also took apart any old clothes, unpicked them and restyled them; nothing was wasted. Fortunately, she only charged a little money and made some very pretty clothes for us.

The climate in Algiers is a very pleasant one; it is warm so we did not have to buy thick, expensive clothing. There was a daily market nearby where one could buy cheap fresh food and we also had some land where we grew fruit and vegetables and kept chickens and rabbits. Compared to children in France, we did at least, have plenty of food. Our education was not disrupted as we went to a French school that taught the recognised syllabus. The language spoken in Algiers is French, so our lives continued much as normal.

We heard that our home in Paris had been taken over by the Germans and used as a club for the officers. We also heard that people in Paris were very short of food and that there were Germans everywhere. People were worried in case they were taken away for breaking some rule. Life was very difficult for ordinary people, they just did not know what would happen next. We also heard that Hitler had insisted that buildings in Paris should not be destroyed. He had always been impressed by the architecture in the city and was determined that it should be preserved at all costs.

We could listen to the wireless, so we were kept informed of life in France and what was happening with the war. We just wondered how it could ever end.

Eventually in 1942, the British and Americans landed in Algiers and from that time we had regular bombing raids by the Germans. The British and American soldiers were very kind to children and gave us chocolate and sweets. We were just fortunate that we didn't live under the occupation with the fear of being arrested or being taken away and being separated from our family. We were also very lucky that my father was not killed or injured and we could be reunited at the end of the war. When we returned to Paris we were so pleased to find our home still standing and not badly damaged.

Paula married an Englishman, she has a daughter and two grandchildren. She is a widow and lives in France.

Jan – 2 years old: Newport, Isle of Wight, England

I was very young at the beginning of the war. My father was in the regular army and before he went away we moved to Newport on the Isle of Wight to be near relatives. Up until war was declared, our family moved around the country to be with him. He left us on the Island in 1939 and we didn't see him again for six years. He fought at Dunkirk, where he was badly wounded and left for dead. Some nuns found him and took him, together with other wounded soldiers, to safety in their convent. After a few days, the Germans came to the convent and took away my father and the two other wounded soldiers.

Fortunately, he was taken to a German hospital where a very skilled doctor removed the shrapnel in his face and also operated on his badly damaged eye. This German surgeon couldn't save his eye, but he undoubtedly saved his life. Eventually, he recovered enough to be sent to a POW camp in the East of Germany. Later, he and other soldiers attempted to escape, but were caught and returned to the camp. A few days later he was taken out to be shot but, at the last minute, a senior German officer came out, stopped the shooting and sent him back to his comrades. No reason was ever given, but whilst waiting he heard bagpipes playing and always thought that they had saved his life. When he asked why he had been saved no one gave him a satisfactory reason.

My mother was informed that he had been killed in action. She realised that she was then the breadwinner and took on three jobs to give us enough money to live. When she went to work in the evening, my older brother would put my sister and I to bed and look after us. We listened to the wireless and played board games such as Ludo and Snakes and Ladders. As we got older we played Monopoly.

In our garden, we grew fruit and vegetables and kept chickens, which were invaluable both for eggs then meat. We also kept rabbits for food, though I always thought of them as pets.

My mother then, to her surprise, had a postcard from the Red Cross, it just said that my father was in a POW camp and was safe! We really celebrated that day. My mother made a cake, everyone was so happy and it was good to see my mother smiling. I couldn't remember my father, but we had his photo and every day my mother would point to the man in the photo and say 'this is your father'.

I can remember the siren going, putting a coat over my nightie and running to a communal shelter at the end of the street. The planes were usually heading for Portsmouth and the dockyard. We always worried that a stray bomb would drop on us. Occasionally, a plane returning to Germany had some bombs left over, which they would release onto the island.

One day we were playing in the street and we saw a soldier walking towards us carrying a kit bag, he didn't stop or speak to us. A few minutes later, my brother came running over to us and told my sister and I to come home straight away as our dad had returned home. We didn't recognise him, he was very thin and his face looked quite different from the photo, which had been taken just before he went away.

Although he couldn't eat very much, my father was always cheerful and very positive. He had been given a medical discharge from the army as he only had one eye. He was demobbed and given five shillings and a new suit. He was very sad and disappointed that his time in the army was over. He had enjoyed army life and had always thought he would stay in the army until retirement.

He managed to get a job driving German PoWs to work at various farms on the island. These men stayed on the island for quite a long time after the war ended before being repatriated.

During the war years we didn't have many toys, everything was difficult to obtain and was expensive. One Christmas, I was given a lovely doll with clothes knitted by my mother, the only problem was she had to keep her hat on to cover up the hole on top of her head. I loved that doll, even though it was clearly second hand.

My war was easy compared to a lot of children, we always had food and, as a family, we stayed together. Fortunately, my father did come back to us, battered but still alive and he was able to work and be part of the family again.

Jan is a widow; she lives in Spain and was married to a regular in the army. She has three children several grandchildren and great grandchildren.

Pam – 7 years old: London, England

I was 7 years old when the war began. We were living in London at the time. My father was a regular sailor in the Royal Navy. Before the war, he had retired at the age of 38, but he re-joined when war was declared.

In 1940, I was given a day off school to go to the theatre in the West End with my mother and a cousin. Not only was this a great treat, but it was possibly my first really lucky escape. That day, at lunchtime, when the children were in the playground, a German plane had flown low over the school. The children were all excited and waved to the pilot. He returned and shot at them and bombed the school. It was terrible, the school was very badly damaged and so many of the children were killed. They were actually buried in a mass grave, I have no idea how many lost their lives, but I think it was about thirty. A most terrible incident which I can never forget.

We then suffered in the Blitz, so my mother decided that London was too dangerous a place for us to be. I had rheumatic fever at the time and, as I was an only child, my mother didn't want me to be evacuated. We went to Marlow and we walked the streets until we found some people who would take us in. We stayed there until the bombing settled down. It was not a very nice place and my mother was treated as an unpaid servant. These people just did not want their lives disrupted, but felt they had to support the war effort. We tried to go back to London, however most of our street had been demolished and our home had been ruined.

Meanwhile, my father had come back to Portsmouth for some leave and we went to see him. We stayed on nearby Hayling Island. One beautiful morning, we took a picnic and went down to the part of the beach that was still open to the public. Most beaches at this time were mined and closed to everyone. Suddenly, my mother saw a German aircraft coming towards us at speed and very low. She grabbed me and we ran for shelter under the jetty which, fortunately, was close by. This was lucky as the plane machine-gunned all along the beach. If we had stayed where we were, we would certainly have been killed. When my dad's leave was up we returned to London. The next day, we heard that the house we had rented in Hayling Island had been bombed and everyone in it had been killed. That was my third life gone.

We returned to Marlow and heard that my father's ship had been torpedoed. He and another sailor spent several days on a raft before being rescued. Eventually, they were picked up by a British ship and taken to the hospital at Greenwich. After they had recovered, they were given a week's leave before being sent back to sea. As he was leaving, he said 'I won't be coming back from this one'. He never returned and we never saw him again. My father's friend told us that he owned a house in Liverpool which was empty and suggested that we should use it. We gratefully took up his offer and went up on the train.

My mother was very nervous and was so pleased to have a house in relative safety. The house was at Dingle and the property, in a cobbled street, was a 'two up and two down'. It was small, but we were so happy there and everyone welcomed us. Once again, I went to another school where the children made me feel very safe and welcome. We could actually look over the wall at the bottom of the garden and see submarines. In later life, I have realised that being so close to a submarine base was also dangerous!

One day we were on a ferry on the Mersey, when we saw a large white hospital ship coming in. As it sailed by, we could hear a band playing 'Land of Hope and Glory'. What a moving sight. Whenever I hear that tune I think about the ship and the wounded men on board. Another memorable time was when we were at New Brighton and saw sailors running down the beach to see a submarine coming in.

My schooling was disrupted and I actually went to thirteen schools. However, I was lucky enough to get a scholarship to go to Art School after the war. I think the war made me independent and taught me to appreciate little things and kindness shown by people to virtual strangers.

Pam now lives in Spain with her husband, she has three children and several grandchildren.

Chapter 13

Anne – 9 years old: York, England

When war was declared, I lived in York with my brother and parents. My favourite pastime was reading and I was fortunate to have a plentiful supply of books. My father worked for the Telephone Company and, as this was a protected occupation, he did not have to go away to war. Whenever the siren sounded, we ran to the shelter at the bottom of our garden. It always felt damp and was a very unpleasant experience, but my father said it was the safest place to be. It was only about thirty yards from the house. Most of the time we heard the drone of the planes going over York on their way to bomb Liverpool, Coventry or any other large town manufacturing munitions, or parts for tanks and aeroplanes. I do not think they thought our city worth dropping bombs on. In the morning, we would listen to the news on our wireless and hear about the raids and devastation that had been caused all over the country the night before, and think how lucky we were.

One night however, we heard the planes returning to Germany when there were explosions all round us, one after another, getting louder and louder. Suddenly there was the loudest explosion ever. It seemed to be right on top of us, as if we were the target. The whole shelter seemed to shake and move and it was very frightening. Nobody spoke. After a few minutes, my father said: 'That sounded like our house'. When it was quiet and the 'All Clear' had sounded, we went outside and could see that our house had gone. It was an amazing sight, instead of a house, it was just a pile of rubble. When it was daylight we went up to the remains and, to my great delight, I found my precious workbox. Amazingly, it was not damaged at all; I still have it in my possession. Apart from books, this was my prize possession. There really was very little that we could salvage and it was obvious that we could not stay there.

At the time we were told that pilots, on returning to Germany, just released any bombs that had not been dropped on their target. It was a policy adopted to destroy the morale of the British people. We discovered later that this was actually the Baedeker Raid on York. We were unlucky that our house had a direct hit. Quite close to our home stood the ruins of York Abbey. An enormous piece of its masonry had flown into the air and, with the force of the explosion, had landed in our garden next to our shelter! The following day, my father and I went around York looking at the damage. Everywhere seemed to be so quiet. It was a very strange atmosphere.

To our horror, the beautiful, medieval Guildhall, the pride of York, had been destroyed, but our great Minster was still there. It had been damaged, but the firemen had managed to put out the flames. We felt so relieved to see it still standing. I think the whole of York would have been devastated if it had been destroyed.

My mother was a very practical person, she gathered any clothes and anything that could be salvaged and put them in the car. We then drove out into the countryside on the North Yorkshire moors. We managed to rent a little cottage, which my mother re-named 'Mouse Cottage'. This was because we entered into a constant battle with mice.

That summer, my brother and I had a wonderful two months of freedom. We found little streams, we explored the moors, found and gathered wild fruit and berries. To our surprise we found two deserted railway cottages at Levisham station. The cottages had gardens full of fruit trees, which we harvested, and also the remnants of a vegetable garden. We pulled up potatoes and gathered beans. We found an old bucket and filled it with the fruit and vegetables and then we struggled back. It seemed heavier and heavier the nearer we got to home. It looked so lovely, all filled with the fruit and vegetables. My mother was so pleased when she saw what we had collected. Soon after this we had to leave Mouse Cottage and look for somewhere else to live.

We went into a village and my mother knocked on doors asking if anyone knew of a cottage to rent. One lady said 'you can have mine, I will go and live with my son in his pub'. We were so lucky. Once again we had somewhere to live and to feel safe.

In this area, we also had great freedom and my brother and I once again roamed the moors. Before long my father insisted that my brother Richard must go into York to school every day on the train. He didn't really consider that, as a girl, my education was of a great deal of importance. However, after a while he said that I too must return to school. Every morning I was put on the York train. When my parents had left the station. I opened the door on the opposite side of the carriage and jumped down onto the track, escaping from the train.

Nobody seemed to notice even though this happened most mornings, I think the school just assumed I couldn't get there. Once again I had the freedom to wander and I made friends with the folk who lived in the cottages on the moor. They were always hospitable and welcomed me into their homes. Most of the younger men had joined the services and I think the women enjoyed having a visitor. We would stop and chat over a cup of tea and a piece of cake. On the moor there was an open door policy. The main fear of these women was that

German parachutists would float down from the skies and attack them. I was told that if I saw anything strange, I must run for help immediately.

I met an evacuee from the East End of London who was billeted at the local bakery. Each morning, we went to a nearby farm and stole two or three eggs and Tommy brought bread rolls from the bakery.

We never took more than we needed. The eggs were just lying around the farmyard. We just waited for an egg to be laid, picked it up and escaped into the local woods, where we cooked them in a frying pan on a fire we had made. They tasted wonderful. By this time, we knew how to make a safe fire and the necessity of putting it out completely when we were finished. We were careful not to allow the fire to spread and destroy woodland.

Many years later, I spoke to the farmer's son and told him what we had done. He said they had known what we were doing but they hadn't taken any action as we hadn't done any harm.

This routine went on for nearly two years before my truancy was discovered, then I just had to go back to school. I was well-read as my parents made sure we had access to the classics and I was an avid reader. My teachers were very understanding and helped me to catch up on the lessons I had missed. It just meant that I had extra homework and I had to work very hard.

The area where we lived was a training ground for soldiers prior to going into battle. In the valley there was a bridge where I could crawl under and hide and hear what was going on with the soldiers. They were learning survival skills and basic country craft. I learnt how to use a compass and how to read maps. I also got to know so many of the soldiers and would take them hot tea in a flask in return for cigarettes, which I smoked. At this time I was 13, nobody ever asked why I was not at school. After a while, I could also help them with map reading and the use of a compass. I even learnt how to catch and kill a rabbit, which my mother cooked for our meal. Some of the soldiers came to our cottage for a cup of tea and a homemade biscuit. My mother was always happy to see them and she made them welcome.

When I eventually went back to school I realised I had to work hard to catch up and to pass exams. My time on the moors made me independent. My knowledge of history and literature was good and with a great deal of hard work, I managed to get a scholarship to university where I studied Literature and eventually became an author.

In spite of Ann's early life of crime she became a successful author and active member of the church and community. She lives with her husband in the New Forest.

Chapter 14

Mike – 7 years old: Coventry, England

At the beginning of the war, my brother and I lived in Coventry with our parents and I was a very enthusiastic Wolf Cub. This was exciting, as we were given knives, which were very sharp. We were shown how to use a knife sensibly and we were expected to obey the rules. If you injured yourself or anyone else, the knife would be taken away from you. We were then taught how to whittle a piece of wood safely. We were also taught how to make a 'safe fire' and we had our own first aid kits. As time went on, we learnt basic first aid. We were never mollycoddled but were made aware of the need for safety, both for oneself and for others. We were told that we were junior soldiers and our country was in great peril. We were also told that we should observe and report anything unusual. For example, a small hole in a roof usually indicated an unexploded, incendiary bomb.

As cubs, we would collect silver paper, clean newspapers, metal and even pigswill as part of our war effort. The swill, I have to say, was extremely smelly and we would return home dirty, in need of a bath, and not very popular with my mother. On the other hand, our Cub Master was very pleased with our efforts. We were given responsibility and made to feel important. I think this helped to make us more independent.

As young boys, my younger brother and I wandered around the city freely. One day we could play in a park but the next week 'NO ADMITTANCE' signs would be there. That was when the excitement started. We knew we had to avoid the sentries in the Memorial Park, but we just had to get in to climb the trees, to see what was going on. We discovered that there were a number of tanks and other army vehicles parked there. If we were seen or caught we were escorted out without ceremony and given dire warning. I must say, this did not deter us. In our games, we were always British pilots escaping from the Germans. The ideas came from our comics, which were anti-German, rather ridiculing the Germans and glorifying the British pilots. Our comics were very precious and we could exchange them with those of friends. Comics became a good form of barter. My favourite comic was *Tiny Tim*, with its exciting weekly serial. I really looked forward to that.

Coventry suffered some terrible air raids, which inflicted a great deal of damage. At the beginning of the war, my father had dug a pit for our Anderson shelter but had unfortunately hit an underground spring which caused it to flood. He had to start all over again. The second time he was more successful. Whenever there was a raid, we would run to our shelter, which was also flooded at times and had a musty smell. This was where my brother and I learnt to play chess. By the end of the war, we were both quite competent and used this skill in later life.

In the shelter, we had some light and a little warmth from a make-do system of two plant pots with candles inside. This was not very successful, so we supplemented this with torchlight. Eventually, my father organised electric light, which made life much easier.

At that time, life was very uncertain. If one went into the city centre after an air raid, it was not unusual to find whole streets demolished and the landscape completely changed. One day, Owen Owens opened a brand new store in the city centre. The very next day, it was completely destroyed and just a heap of rubble! Another big store called Bendalls was also bombed, but that soon re-opened in a prefabricated building. The feeling around was that life must carry on as normal. The slogan 'Business as Usual' appeared in many shops. Nobody complained and the determination to win the war was very strong. It did not occur to people that we might even lose. However, after the blitz, morale was low and the king and queen came up to Coventry to give their support and to cheer us all up. People were very moved that they had come to show that they really cared.

Thousands of people died or were wounded and many houses and buildings were just left to burn, as the water mains were broken. Coventry burned for four days. My brother and I went into town after the main Blitz. It was a horrible sight; I saw an arm sticking out of the rubble and immediately called one of the wardens. He just said the people there were dead and it was his job to save the living. We heard people screaming and calling out for help. The police, ambulance people and wardens were so busy doing their best for people; nobody took any notice of us. Even horse drawn carts were used to clear the sites and to take dead and wounded people to hospitals and to the mortuary. It was a very sad time for so many people. Even our famous, beautiful cathedral was in ruins.

We were all very aware that nothing should be wasted and we were always hungry, so we never left any food on our plates. My mother worked hard to give us good wholesome food, which must have been difficult with all the shortages. In our gardens we grew our own fruit and vegetables and kept chickens and rabbits. We learnt very quickly that rabbits and chickens were for food and they were not pets. This was difficult to accept at first, especially as we had given them all names. Milk and some other produce was delivered by horse and cart and, whenever we could, we would collect manure along the street to be used as compost for the garden. Very good for the roses too. This was precious and one had to be quick to collect it before other boys who had the same idea. All free land in the city was cultivated, even land alongside railway lines.

Our clothes did not fit very well and most of the time I remember wearing wellingtons or gym shoes. I think that is why I have had trouble with my feet in later years. We were always being told that we would eventually grow into clothes; I think sometimes the clothes wore out before we grew into them.

As a family, we were always encouraged to be independent. I remember one day, when I was returning from boarding school, I was travelling home on my own on the train. I was 9 at the time. Suddenly, there was an air raid and the train stopped for safety in a tunnel for about half an hour. When it continued, it could not stop at my station as there was bomb damage. It continued for another five miles to the next station, consequently I had to walk five miles home in the dark, along country lanes, carrying a heavy suitcase. After a little while, I decided to hide my suitcase in some bushes and to come back for it next day. When I arrived home, instead of a wonderful welcome, my mother was cross and worried that my suitcase, full of precious clothes may have been stolen! My brother and I went back the next day with a wheelbarrow and it was still there, thank goodness, crisis over.

During the Coventry Blitz, the buses had been very badly damaged and London buses were sent up to help keep the service running, but these were very old and slow. When we were cycling up hill, we used to hold onto the back of a bus and get a free ride and then we raced the bus downhill. We did not see the danger, but the conductors certainly did not approve and would shout obscenities at us.

My uncle had started a factory in Coventry and a story went round that some workmen had put the tip of a German pilot's thumb in a matchbox, which was then passed around the factory. A very unpleasant thing to do, but so many people in Coventry had lost family and friends, and Germans were the enemy. It took a long time for opinions to change. However, years later, Coventry was twinned with Dresden, another city that had suffered terrible bombing during the war.

When the war came to an end in 1945, there were great celebrations on VE Day. There was relief, happiness, and also great sadness for all the people who had been killed or injured. Then they started to rebuild our city and a new cathedral. Very slowly, life got back to normal.

In spite of all the disruption of the war years, I managed to pass my exams for Bablake Grammar School and eventually, that helped me be accepted as a cadet at the Royal Air Force College at Cranwell, to become a pilot in the RAF and thus to continue my exciting life.

Mike now lives in the New Forest with his wife. They are both authors.

Chapter 15

Natalie – 9 years old: Zlin, Czechoslovakia

(This lady asked for her name to be changed)

Natalie lived with her parents and two younger sisters in the beautiful town of Zlin in Czechoslovakia. This was a town that had developed around a shoe factory with a philanthropic owner who looked after his workers in a similar way to Cadbury and Rowntree in the UK. He built houses and sports facilities for his employees. It was a close-knit community, which was part of the Bata family, the international shoe firm, started in the time of Natalie's great grandfather. Most of the workers in the area worked for, and depended upon, this family for their livelihood.

For my family the war started in 1937. My parents became very secretive and I was aware that things were not right. My father kept saying, 'We must be ready', but as children, did not know what we had to be ready for. We just knew our lives were about to change.

My father became increasingly nervous when he heard of the German annexation of Czechoslovakia (the Sudetenland). He decided that it was only a matter of time before the Germans would take over the whole of Czechoslovakia and then we would be completely under German domination. We simply packed a few things and got into the car, as if we were going on a short holiday, and travelled towards the Austrian border. There we found German soldiers stopping cars and arresting people they thought were attempting to leave the country. Everyone seemed very frightened. My father decided that we would have a better chance of escaping if we travelled in a lorry instead of a large car. Somehow we managed to get a lorry. My mother, my two sisters and I climbed into the back and sat on a large heap of hay and made ourselves as comfortable as possible for the long journey ahead. After a short time, we could see a roadblock ahead so we immediately buried ourselves within the hay. When we stopped, two German soldiers thrust pitchforks into the back of the lorry. We had to keep still and absolutely quiet. Fortunately we were not discovered, but it was so very close and frightening. If we had been found we would have been sent away to an internment camp.

My father was very upset and, with a heavy heart, just said we must return to Zlin, so we drove all the way back to our home. My sisters and I were so happy to be back in familiar surroundings and to be able to continue what we thought was normal living. We were so wrong.

A few months later during our summer holidays my parents collected together as much as they could, packed the car, and said we were going to the farm for a holiday. We locked up the house and drove out into the country to the farm we always rented in the summer. I remember feeling worried as no one would tell me when we would be returning home. My father wanted to get us away for a short break, he was afraid for our lives if we stayed in the town. We had a wonderful carefree two months in beautiful countryside, swimming in a river, going for long walks, taking picnics and not thinking about war and other problems. Our main concern however, was that our grandfather had insisted on staying behind on his own in Zlin.

We returned to the city when my parents felt confident that things had calmed down. After the annexation of the Sudetenland into Nazi Germany, the rest of the country was powerless to resist occupation. The Germans had just marched into our country. Most of the local population were against the Germans, but they were threatened that if they did not cooperate, the lives of their families would be in danger. Nobody was safe and there was a feeling that one could not even trust neighbours. A few of them were actually willing to cooperate with the Germans. We lived in constant fear of being reported for any small misdemeanour and there was always the constant fear of a 'knock on the door' and what that would mean.

My mother gathered up clothes and anything we did not need and took them out to the country in exchange for food, such as meat, sacks of flour, fresh vegetables or anything that was available. This helped so much to supplement our meagre rations and to make our meals more enjoyable. By the end of the war we had little left to exchange. After the summer holidays we went back to school. Everything had changed, we were not allowed to speak our own language. We were only allowed to speak German. Whenever anyone entered the classroom, we had to stand up and give the Nazi salute. If you did not lift your arm high enough you were punished. We all had to say 'Heil Hitler'.

Certain subjects such as Czech history and our own language were banned. Only German geography post 1937 was allowed (this was when Germany annexed the Sudetenland and occupied Czechoslovakia). We were not permitted to have meetings of any kind and the curfew was very strict.

One day when we were in our classroom, the door crashed open and two Nazi officers burst in. We all stood up said and 'Heil Hitler' and the Nazis went up to our teacher and shouted something in German. She answered in Czech and one of them just took out his pistol and shot her twice in the head in front of all of us. Then he put his gun away and they both left the classroom without saying a word. She lay on the floor covered in blood. We all just stood there not moving, not saying anything until one girl began to cry. With that everyone started to cry, another teacher came in and took us all out of the room and into the school hall. This horrific event happened on a Friday morning and we were all sent home and told not to come back until Monday. We could not believe that this had happened, our teacher had always been popular, she was always helpful and kind.

We were told later that she was Jewish and had been working against the country. We discovered that a pupil from our class had reported her for speaking to the class in Czech. One could not talk or say anything that could be misinterpreted as being a Partisan sympathiser or anti-Nazi. This was strictly forbidden.

Sometimes the Germans would come to the school and order us to go into the woods to collect herbs. These would be weighed and, if we had not collected enough, we would be sent out to get more. We also had to collect clean newspapers, which were weighed. We spent our days being frightened in case we were punished or taken away.

We watched helplessly as the Germans rounded up Jews. The soldiers would go into a block of flats, bring out families and round them up, herding them into lorries. The soldiers pushed, shoved and hit anyone who was slow or old. We just heard screams and crying as they were taken away and we never heard or saw them again. One day I decided to visit a school friend who was Jewish. When I arrived at her block of flats I saw a lorry outside and several German soldiers all holding guns, talking and laughing. I went to the large open door and was surprised to see my friend being dragged down several flights of stairs by her long, blond hair. By the time they arrived at the foot of the stairs, there was blood everywhere and she was dead. We were both 12 years old. There was nothing I could do about it. I was helpless and just stood there hoping not be noticed. I watched them take away the rest of her family. Nobody took any notice of me and I just walked away in shock.

In those days people did dreadful things. We never knew whom we could trust, who we could talk to or what we could say in case it could be used against us or our family.

The Germans told my father and grandfather that the factory would be required to make shoes and boots for the German Army. They also said that if they refused, they would be shot and their families would be sent to Dachau or Auschwitz. My father and grandfather decided to keep the factory working, giving so many people the chance to work and to be able to feed their families. They knew that if they refused they would be shot and replaced by Nazi 'puppets'.

My uncle was accused of being a Partisan sympathiser and anti-Nazi. He was well known locally and the Nazis decided to make an example of him. They sent him to Dachau concentration camp. My parents tried to support his family but we never heard from him or saw him again. It was a terrible time for everyone.

My father would disappear for a few days at a time. It was only after the war that we learnt that he was part of a partisan group working against the 'puppet' government and the Nazi occupation. They did a lot of damage and their lives were always in danger. Sometimes, a person would report people to the Germans in a desperate attempt to save their own lives or those of their families. Czechoslovakia was, in those days, a mixture of Nazis, communists, police – some who were of German extraction – collaborators, and people who were loyal to the Czech Government in exile. We were always relieved when my father was at home and just going to work every day.

We believed that once the Germans retreated life would be much better, but we had not considered the Russians, who we thought were liberating us. Life was, if possible, worse than ever. As they approached they did terrible things and we would hear of people being raped. The Russians did not approve of the factory being in private ownership. We were turned out of our house and, although we found a cottage to live in, we were totally under their control. A Russian general took over our home. At least we were not vandalised, the general always had guards looking after the property. The soldiers were very ignorant men. They took our bicycles from the cellar (we were not allowed to take them with us) and just rode over the garden, not respecting the lovely surroundings, and broke the bikes. The Germans did not do that. The general insisted that my father would go to see him at 8am every day to give a detailed report from the factory about the boots and shoes he needed for the Russian Army. It was almost impossible to be able to fulfil these orders on time, and there were always threats. The Russians did not agree with the factory being a family business, but they needed the boots and shoes that were being made and decided to use the expertise of the workforce.

My father decided that we would have to leave and go to the West somehow. He told us that we would only be able to take one bag and that we must not tell anyone of our plans. The first time we planned this, someone reported us to the police who came and asked lots of questions, but fortunately, my father managed to persuade them we were only going away for a weekend. I think he had to pay them money to go away and leave us alone. The next attempt was more carefully planned. This was in September 1947, a date imprinted on my memory. I was at that time a medical student in Prague. I came back to Zlin to be with the family.

We were well organised, bribes had been paid in advance to get papers and we had a route well planned. We had arranged to pick up a lorry in the countryside. My mother, my two sisters and I got into the back, covered by a blanket and a tarpaulin and lots of fruit. This was how we had to travel. We knew if we were stopped we couldn't move or make a sound. We came to a checkpoint and were stopped and the soldiers looked into the back of the lorry. My father got out of the cab and offered the soldiers some fruit and vegetables to keep them happy and to distract them. They did not look any more and told us to keep going. My father had paid a man in advance to put large planks of wood across a small river so that the lorry could cross over.

When we got there, in the middle of the night, we found there were no planks of wood. Either the man had taken the wood away or he had not put them there at all. We got out of the lorry, left it and started off on foot. It was cold and very dark and we had to move quietly and quickly. We had to wade across a small river to avoid patrols of police or Russian soldiers. We could not waste any time, as we had to cross the border into Germany at a specific time when it would be safe.

The next day we actually crossed the border, avoiding the guards with their dogs and, much to our relief, we found ourselves in the American zone of Germany. We were very quickly handed over to the Red Cross and we were taken to a camp full of displaced persons. We were classed as displaced persons and we stayed in the camp for four months.

Eventually, my father and I were allowed to take a train to the British Consul in Munich, where we managed to get the necessary papers for us to go to England. We went through Holland by train and then by boat. It was such a relief that we were all safe and, although we had lost everything, we could start our lives anew in a free country. It took many years for me to stop being suspicious, and there are still some events that I will never forget.

Natalia married a fellow Czech and had three children. She is a widow and still lives in England. Her war lasted longer than most as it continued until her family escaped from Russian occupation.

Chapter 16

June – 4 years old: Guernsey, Channel Islands

The First World War did not touch Guernsey and the UK Government had hoped the same would happen in 1939. They were aware that the islands would be very difficult, if not impossible, to defend once the German Army had invaded and occupied France. When the Germans invaded Holland, Belgium and Luxembourg, it was decided that it was the time to evacuate children and people who were not island born.

I was 4 years old when war was declared and my parents decided that my mother and I should be evacuated to England to stay with relatives. This was a very difficult decision as my mother wanted to stay in Guernsey with my father. We packed our cases and set off for the harbour in St Peter Port where I fell and hurt myself. We returned home and then my parents decided that we could all go together, as a family, the following day. My fall was to change our lives for the next five years.

The next day, 28 June 1940, German planes bombed and machine-gunned the ships and little boats in St Peter Port. Over forty-four people were killed and many more were injured. We had no warning of this and people could not believe what was happening. Everyone just ran for shelter. On the quayside there were carts and lorries loaded with tomatoes and flowers ready to be shipped to England. Our beautiful harbour had been transformed. Everywhere seemed to be ablaze and smoking. It was a terrible sight and one we had certainly not anticipated.

This made it impossible for us to go to England, the decision had been made for us. We had to stay. Hitler had heard of the demilitarisation of the islands and decided to invade.

On 30 June, German soldiers landed at our little airport and marched straight down to the harbour to accept the surrender of the island from the Bailiff at the Royal Hotel. That was when the Nazi German flag was raised on our island and it remained there for five years.

Fortunately, on 20 June, children who were of school age had been given the option of being evacuated to England with their school. This was a difficult decision for parents to make as they had no idea where their children were going or who they would be living with. Actually, they only had four hours to make this important decision. They also knew that if the islands were invaded it would be impossible to contact them until the war was over. Most young men of fighting age had already left to join one of the services.

On the whole, the Germans behaved quite well towards children and were fairly kind to them. However they believed in strict discipline. If a child misbehaved punishment was harsh. We had a German officer who was a meteorologist billeted in our home. Every morning he went to the officers' mess and brought back food. He always took more food than he needed. He would leave some bread and butter and say to my mother 'give it to the kinder'. He was always polite and pleasant to our family.

Most people were wary of the Germans because they were never sure how they would react. If their rules were obeyed you were safe, but if you digressed, punishment could be hard and one could be sent to a prison on Guernsey or an internment camp in France or Germany. They set curfews and regulations, had their own law enforcement and introduced European time to the island. They also used their own currency. The Germans left the everyday running of the island to the Controlling Committee, which was led by His Majesty's Attorney and the Bailiff.

We did not have any armed resistance on the island as there was nowhere for anyone to hide or disappear to in such a small place. However, passive resistance continued throughout the occupation. People disobeyed orders, helped the slave labour and produced anti-Nazi leaflets. Several young men were caught doing this and were sent away to concentration camps. Some never returned. One or two escaped to England, but this was very dangerous. If they had been caught they would certainly have been shot.

The Germans insisted that the German language was taught in schools. They used this as an excuse to spread Nazi propaganda. We were told that it was only a matter time before Germany occupied England and Hitler replaced the king as head of state. Every so often, British planes flew over the islands dropping leaflets with up-to-date news from England telling us the true state of the war. Children found the leaflets and took them home or brought them into school.

A story was told of a young boy who climbed a tree to retrieve a leaflet. Unfortunately, when he climbed down he found a German soldier waiting for him. The soldier took the leaflet but he did not report the incident. These leaflets were forbidden. The boy had been lucky.

The people of Guernsey felt cut off. There were no letters, magazines or English newspapers and wireless news was forbidden. We were not allowed to have wireless sets, but all over the island people had hidden sets. They listened to broadcasts and then passed on all the latest BBC news, a very dangerous thing to do.

There was a great shortage of food. Although we had ration books there was still not enough food and people were starving. All medical supplies came from France and after 'D-Day' it was much worse, as no supplies came to the island. The Germans also had difficulty in managing their supplies of food.

We lived in the country and grew vegetables and fruit, but sometimes we found that people had helped themselves at night. Everyone was so hungry and looking for food. In the town, people found it even more difficult. Sometimes children followed a lorry taking potatoes and vegetables to the German barracks and picked up anything that fell off. Occasionally, a German soldier felt sorry for them and gave them one or two potatoes to take home.

Fishing boats were allowed to go out if they had a permit from the Germans, but an armed guard always accompanied them out to sea. The Germans were worried in case the men escaped and sailed away to England.

My grandfather was a butcher and, on occasion, went to a farm to slaughter an animal illegally. He was paid in meat and usually wrapped the joint in a blanket and put it on his bike trailer. The punishment for this offence was deportation to France or Germany. Fortunately, he was never stopped by any soldiers.

The International Red Cross certainly saved many people from starving. The Red Cross ship the SS *Viga* sailed from Lisbon six times with essential supplies of flour, medical supplies and food parcels for families. The food parcels came from New Zealand and Canada and included soap, chocolate and other goods that were unavailable on the island. People looked forward to these parcels, which were always gratefully received. The German soldiers had been ordered not to touch the parcels. They were threatened by their officers with being shot or deported if caught stealing. Some were so hungry that they broke into houses to steal food. My mother actually hid the parcels at the back of the piano and my father kept an iron pole near to the bed, which he always said was to hit anyone who broke in. We were so grateful to the brave sailors who brought us these supplies. Even to his day I find it amazing that the neutrality of this ship was recognised.

Occasionally, British planes flew over to bomb a strategic target. One day I was out when a British plane flew over. I had been told that if a wall or a hedge was nearby to stay very close to avoid flying shrapnel. A passing German officer grabbed me and took me into a nearby house. He told me always to be careful and to keep safe. German soldiers were constantly afraid that if they committed any offence, they might be sent to the Eastern Front. Some even injured themselves to avoid being sent away.

On the island there were PoWs from Russia and Eastern Europe. The Germans had transported these men as slave labour and they were treated very badly. They were in Guernsey to build fortifications and a railway line to transport concrete and materials to improve and extend the airfield, which was then a Luftwaffe camp. They were dressed in rags and had more rags wound around their feet instead of shoes. Nobody was allowed to help these poor wretches and anyone caught defying this law was either deported or given a prison sentence. Some were caught trying to help them and they were sent away never to return. A Russian pilot, who was one of the slaves, was hidden by a lady who was eventually arrested by the Germans. She was sent to Ravensbruck concentration camp never to return. A man then hid the pilot until liberation (he is still alive today and appeared in a recent TV programme about the island in the war years).

Eventually the Guernsey press informed us that the war was coming to an end and we could fly the red, white and blue of the Union Jack on 8 May 1945. The whole population was excited and, for the first time in five years, turned their wireless sets on loud to heard Winston Churchill saying 'our dear Channel Islands will be free'. At this time nobody worried if the Germans heard the news. This was when the Nazi flag was lowered and our own flag raised once again.

My mother used some red, white and blue material to make me a new dress. We knew ships were sailing toward the islands. Many people stood on the cliffs watching for the ships approaching from England. Everyone rushed to the harbour to see the flotilla of ships and then the British soldiers. What a sight when they came ashore with their rifles and bayonets! Everyone was cheering, laughing and hugging anyone nearby. The soldiers gave us sweets and the adults cigarettes. Both soldiers and islanders were overcome with emotion and relief. Peace had come at last! The rest of the day was just one great party with singing and dancing in the streets. We went into a bunker and looked through a gun sight. To our amazement, we could see the faces of people in St Peter Port, which was two miles away. The celebrations went on for a week.

At long last the German occupation of our island was over The German soldiers were now prisoners of war, most of them were sent to prisoner of war camps in England, some stayed behind to help the British soldiers clear up land mines and to dismantle the large guns. Then, we just had to wait for children, fathers and islanders to return and be reunited. Some islanders did not return from the concentration camps and some young men were killed fighting in the services. Even to this day, we celebrate Liberation Day.

My parents were very protective toward me during the war, although I was very young I never felt frightened or threatened and moved around freely. People on the island helped each other as much as possible. Everyone felt they all shared the same difficulties and problems. We all had regarded Winston Churchill as our 'Hero' and knew that one day we would be free and reunited with our loved ones.

As a family, we were very fortunate that all family members returned safely after the war.

After the war, a young girl called Mollie Bihet wrote to Winston Churchill from the people of Guernsey thanking him for liberating the islands. She was so thrilled to have a reply from Downing Street signed by Winston. The local paper printed her letter and the reply and I am sure she still treasures the letter.

In June the king and queen visited Guernsey and twenty island children went to London to take part in the Victory Parade. All schoolchildren on the island were given a 'Liberation Day' medal.

June is an author and lives on Guernsey. She is still writing books.

German tank entering Prague 1939. (IWM)

Occupation of Guernsey 1939. (IWM)

A poster informing the public that special trains were running to take evacuees to safe destinations, 1939. (IWM)

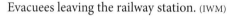

EVACUATION
OF
WOMEN AND CHILDREN FROM LONDON, Etc.

FRIDAY, 1st SEPTEMBER.

Up and Down business trains as usual, with few exceptions.

Main Line and Suburban services will be curtailed while evacuation is in progress during the day.

SATURDAY & SUNDAY, SEPTEMBER 2nd & 3rd.

The train service will be exactly the same as on Friday.

Remember that there will be very few Down Mid-day business trains on Saturday.

SOUTHERN RAILWAY

Evacuees leaving the railway station. (IWM)

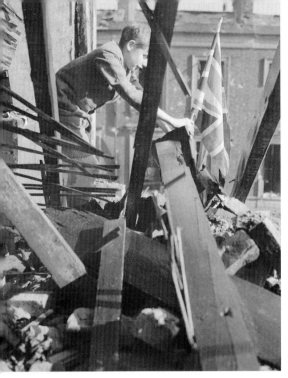

Boy displaying the Union Jack, London 1940. Patriotic signs like this helped to maintain morale. (IWM)

Young boy entering an Anderson Shelter, carrying his gas mask, London 1940. (IWM)

School girls sitting on the wing of a German aircraft that had recently crashed, 1940. (IWM)

Children in Coventry searching for books after their school had been bombed, 10 April 1941. (IWM

Evacuees in the country, 1941. (IWM)

Angela with her two brothers outside their home in Virginia Water, London 1942. (Angela Dowland)

Bomb damage in Valletta, Malta, 1 May 1942. (IWM)

A young messenger wearing a tin hat outside an ARP post. (IWM)

Children continuing their lessons in an air raid shelter. (IWM)

15-year-old girl delivering milk. (IWM)

Red Cross parcels delivered to starving people in the Channel Islands by the SS *Viga*. (IWM)

Girls from the Hitler Youth (including Hilde) enjoying an activity weekend in the forest. (Hilde Reucroft)

German school girls, members of the Hitler youth in North Germany 1943. (Hilde Reucroft)

Girl Guides, 1944. (IWM)

Children waving flags on VE Day. (IWM)

The Norwegian royal family return to
Oslo on HMS *Norfolk* 6 June 1945. (IWM)

Evacuees returning home after the war. (IWM)

Chapter 17

Maria – 4 years old: Malta

M alta, being a small island in the Mediterranean, has been the subject of sieges and occupations for nearly 2,000 years. It has always held an important strategic position. The island's first siege was in 1565 and the last was the Great Siege of 1942.

I was 4 years old when the Second World War was declared. I lived in a village called Naxxar with my father, mother, brothers and sisters. My mother was always busy, so my eldest sister looked after us. We always had to do what she said.

My father left on his bicycle early each day to go to work in a brewery and returned late in the evening.

When war in Europe was declared, we knew that Winston Churchill was determined that the island must be defended at all cost. Every morning before school, we listened to the wireless on Redifusion Malta, so we were aware of what was going on in mainland Europe. Everybody talked about the war with Germany. We knew that Britain would try to defend us, but we were also aware that Britain was a long way away and Italy, Germany's main ally, was very close to Malta. Everyone seemed to be talking and worrying about the future. At that time, the Royal Air Force had Gladiator fighter planes and one or two Hurricanes stationed on one of the three airfields on the island. The Gladiators were old biplanes, three of which were fondly referred to as 'Faith, Hope, and Charity'. The Royal Navy had several large war ships in Grand Harbour.

In the early days we watched the planes take off, climb up into the blue sky and attack and repulse Italian reconnaissance planes. Each day they returned triumphant and we felt a great sense of relief. They flew low over our school on their approach to their airfield. We watched them from our playground and we all cheered when we saw them return safely. At that time it seemed exciting, but that was before the bombing started.

Each morning we had a practice at school to make sure we knew what to do if we had an air raid. Some sensible boys were chosen to turn the handle of a machine, which made a loud, whining noise. This got louder and louder and we were told that if one heard that sound, we had to go to the nearest shelter immediately. Malta did not need to build many shelters; we were very lucky to have large underground tunnels all over the island. In the early days, when the sirens sounded, most people from the village went into these tunnels, which were cold, dark, and miserable. Children just sat on the floor crying and shouting and many of the women just said prayers with their rosaries. As time progressed, we realised that we might have to spend a lot of our time in these tunnels. Things improved when people took stools, old chairs, blankets and rugs to sit on. They also took oil lamps and candles. My mother always had some food and drink in case we were there for a long time. When the 'All Clear' sounded the children became alive, all wanting to go to the toilet and complaining they were hungry.

On 11 June 1940 we had our first air raid by the Italians. Luckily, this did not do a great deal of damage and did not last long.

Every day I walked to school with my sister. If there was an air raid the nuns would usher us into a shelter, which was another tunnel. It was such a noisy place, we could hear children crying or talking and we could hear the bombs dropping all over the island. Before long, the Germans took over the bombing and then it was intense. They bombed relentlessly, hoping either to obliterate our island or to force us into surrender. The underground shelters saved so many lives. After the war, we were told that Malta had over 3,000 raids in two years, and that over 30,000 buildings had been either badly damaged or destroyed. In April 1942, thirty-six times more bombs fell on Malta than had fallen on Coventry during the blitz. I think we spent more time in the shelters than outside.

Malta is a small island, so the bombing was never far away; one constantly heard explosions and the thud of bombs. However, the Grand Harbour at Valletta and the airfields were their prime targets. We had bombing both in the daytime and also at night, so we were all very tired; but however tired we were, we still had to go to school the next day.

In the town of Mosta, the beautiful cathedral with its great dome took a direct hit. By some miracle the bomb, a very large one, did not explode. It was later defused and remains in the cathedral to this day, as a reminder of those dark days. When the cathedral was saved, my mother said it was an omen of good luck, and God was on our side.

We had an uncle living with us who hated going into the shelter. He always refused to come with us when he heard the siren. He just hated the noise. However, one day my mother insisted that he should come with us. That day, our village was badly damaged and when we went back to our house we found the ceiling and furniture had come down into our sitting room. If my uncle had stayed in the house, he would almost certainly have been killed. He had a lucky escape and after that, he always came into the shelter. Fortunately, we had our house repaired quickly and we did not have to look for somewhere else to live.

We had ration books for basic food, things like pasta, rice, flour and sugar. We were lucky that we lived in a village with a large garden in which we grew fruit and vegetables. We also kept chickens, pigeons and rabbits. We all helped my mother with the garden and I enjoyed looking for eggs and feeding the chickens and rabbits. My mother used to barter spare eggs for other food. People living in towns were very short of food and were happy to buy any spare produce. Before too long everything was in short supply and eventually there was no Kerosene oil for fuel, so we went out looking for pieces of wood to burn. Every tree on the island disappeared and people even burned furniture.

Victory Kitchens opened to help those who were close to starving. Volunteers cooked a nutritious stew or a thin vegetable soup on a daily basis. People may have had food, but they had no means of cooking it. They were very hungry and were happy to pay six pence for a pot of vegetable stew or three pence for a thin soup; sometimes there would be some pasta or rice added.

It then looked as if the Germans were trying to starve us into surrender. When people thought they could go on no longer, a vital convoy of ships from England arrived in Valletta with precious food supplies and also a tanker with much needed fuel for the aircraft and some fuel for cooking. When we saw them dock, we all went down to the harbour and cheered, knowing we had been saved from starvation. People were so happy; it was wonderful. We were told later that several ships had been sunk on their way to Malta. After that, other ships got through to bring us precious supplies.

The shops were nearly depleted of goods to sell. As a family, we were lucky that my mother made our clothes and could adapt them to hand down to my brothers and sisters. I was always happy to have handed-down clothes.

Travelling around the island was not easy, so most of the time we walked or went by bicycle. Occasionally there was a bus. When my mother had a baby, the midwife came to the house on a bicycle. Doctors and some service-men were the only ones with cars.

In 1942, King George VI awarded the George Cross to the island. The citation was 'to honour the brave people of the island'. The honour had never been awarded to any other island or country before. We were very proud to have received this decoration, it was so good that the bravery of the islanders had been recognised by the king.

We heard on the wireless that 7 May 1945 would be VE day. It was such a happy day. All over the island, in towns and villages, bands played, church bells rang and in Valletta, there was the noise of ships' sirens in Grand Harbour.

Flags appeared and were put up, the Union Jacks, Maltese flags and local flags, the people of Malta love their flags! Everyone had a party, everybody was talking to friends and strangers alike. Everywhere there was dancing and singing in the streets. People found it hard to believe that the war was really over.

There were ruins everywhere, but the cathedral in Valletta survived. Britain sent money and materials to help with the reconstruction of our island and to rebuild our economy.

Shops reopened and life gradually returned to normal. Once again, the colourful Maltese buses could be seen all over the island. We then had to wait for loved ones to return from the war and to start living in a peaceful way, once more.

Maria married an Englishman and lives in England with her husband. They have three grown up daughters.

Chapter 18

Geoffrey – 10 years old: crossing the Atlantic, on board the SS *Fanad Head*

In the summer holidays of 1939, my father was offered a lecture tour of the USA and Canada. Although there was a great deal of war preparation going on I think, secretly, that people felt it would blow over, and my parents thought the chance of a month's holiday in the USA and Canada could not be missed. It all sounded very exciting.

We were due to return to the UK on 2 of September. I was travelling with my parents and my two brothers. My father had decided that we should return on a cargo ship; this was partly because it was less expensive but also, he thought, it would be an adventure for three young boys. We did not realise just how exciting it was going to be!

We were in Montreal and were surprised to find everyone so excited, chattering, running everywhere and saying that war in Europe was imminent. There appeared to be a great deal of confusion. The main buildings were guarded by soldiers, who all appeared very serious. There were crowds outside newspaper offices waiting for the latest news. A man would come out regularly and pin up the latest bulletin in French. Suddenly, a bulletin was pinned up saying that Great Britain and France were waiting for a formal decision from Germany and, if they did not hear, we would be at war with Germany. Naturally, my parents were very concerned about this situation.

The ship, the SS *Fanad Head* was due to leave on 3 September, so we all went aboard on the evening of the second. The next morning, very early, we were woken up by a steward, who informed us that Great Britain and France were at war with Germany. He also said that if we wanted to leave the ship they would understand. There were only three other passengers; nobody opted to leave.

We got up and went to the dining room where we ate a magnificent breakfast, then my brothers and I had a walk around to explore the ship. It all seemed so exciting to us, so different from our normal ordered life at home. She was quite a large ship of 5,200 tons. On the funnel she had a white shield embossed with a red hand. We sailed down the river, passing a brand new

American destroyer and several other ships. As we passed Quebec it was getting dark and misty, the town looked like something out of a fairy tale with all the lights glistening. We went to bed and slept soundly. Nobody spoke about the war.

Next day, we left our pilot behind and carried on with our journey, out to the wide, open sea and into the vast Atlantic Ocean.

It soon became obvious that the crew were preparing for war. The first sign was the typewritten notes that appeared in our cabins saying that passengers must not smoke on the deck or use torches at night. The portholes were all to be painted black and we were to ensure that they were shut at night, so that not even a chink of light could be seen from outside. We also had to put black paper on the inside of the porthole. We were told we must keep cheerful at all times! My father said 'how very British!'

Most of the ship was being painted battleship grey as we sailed along and the lifeboats were overhauled. Everyone on board got down to work and helped the crew with their efforts. By 13 September, nearly all the work had been completed and that was when we entered, what the captain said, was the danger zone. Every night we listened to the news report from Daventry and we heard some disturbing reports. Apparently, some U-boats had just torpedoed merchant ships without any warning, whilst others had actually towed lifeboats to the nearest neutral ship or port!

On 14 September we went to breakfast as usual, when we heard the ship's bells ringing and people were running everywhere. The captain had spotted a submarine on the starboard bow about five miles away. It was approaching us at top speed. We all went up on deck and put our lifejackets on. The ship altered its course, but we were no match for the superior engines on the submarine and after an hour and a half the captain decided that we should abandon ship.

The boats were lowered and we were aware that the submarine was firing shells; we could hear the noise as the shells passed across our bows!

While this was going on, our wireless operator was busy sending out SOS messages to two shore bases and an American ship. The aircraft carrier *Ark Royal* heard our SOS and signalled that she was coming to our aid. We were told to take extra blankets with us as it gets very cold at night in an open boat. We climbed down a rope ladder to get into our lifeboat. This was very difficult, but we escaped injury and were all lucky that we managed without any casualties, despite not having had any practice.

The sailors in our boat rowed away from the ship and, to our amazement, the U-boat came alongside and their captain spoke to our captain.

The submarine was a very modern one; it was painted khaki green with a large, black swastika behind the conning tower. It was armed with two guns. Some of the crew came up on deck, they all looked very young. They were interested to see who we were. In perfect English, the captain said it was unfortunate for us that his submarine was much faster than our boat and he was interested to know the nature of our cargo. He seemed very surprised when we told him that it was grain (he had expected it to be munitions). I think he had believed we were a naval ship. He told us that he had alerted an American boat in the area and she was coming to our aid.

He then told us that he was going to destroy our ship. The submarine partially submerged and travelled over to our ship, which they boarded. Fortunately, our captain had destroyed all papers and codes.

It was very unpleasant in the lifeboat, we were rocking and wallowing and everyone was feeling very seasick, my brother even refused a sweet, which was unheard of.

We stayed like this for some time when we heard the hum of an aeroplane coming towards us. I had always been interested in aircraft recognition and realised this was a Skua dive bomber, used by the Fleet Air Arm. The plane dropped four bombs as the U-boat submerged, it carried on and dropped another three bombs and then it disappeared behind the ship. We never saw it again and thought it must have crashed into the sea, or somehow flown back to its ship, without us seeing it. Ten minutes later another Skua came and signalled 'help coming'. Our wireless operator signalled back with a hand torch. Suddenly, the submarine reappeared and the Skua dived towards it and we heard the noise of gunfire from them both, unfortunately the aircraft then nose-dived into the sea.

Soon after, six biplanes arrived and circled, searching for the submarine. Everyone in the boats was cheering, seasickness had been forgotten. Then we saw a great plume of smoke and realised our ship had been hit by a torpedo from the submarine. The planes saw the track of the torpedo and this gave away the position of the U-boat. According to Geoffrey's diary, the planes 'swooped down like a lot of hungry gulls after bread' and dropped many bombs. We could see the explosions. Our poor ship started to break up, the masts slowly canted towards each other, then the funnel gradually sank into the water and the boilers exploded one after the other. The bow and stern then rose slowly out of the sea and disappeared forever. All was gone in a few seconds. It was quite an emotional moment for our captain, the crew and for us. We had been drifting in the lifeboats for eight hours.

We looked up and saw smoke on the horizon and before long, we realised two destroyers were sailing towards us at full speed. It was an emotional time and my mother had tears in her eyes.

Apparently, the destroyers had travelled 200 miles at top speed to find us. When they arrived, the first destroyer circled around looking for the U-boat. The second came to a standstill near enough for us to row alongside, they threw us lines to make fast. We struggled up a rope ladder onto the deck of HMS *Tartar*. I found it much more difficult to climb up the rope ladder than it had been getting down into the lifeboat. However, we all managed it, our only loss was my mother's shoe. The sailors were so kind and we were given hot soup and told to relax in the wardroom. The captain even gave my mother his cabin. This was such a special, exciting time for my brothers and I.

The next day we joined *Ark Royal* and sailed towards Scotland. On the way, we saw the remains of another ship, the SS *Athenia*, it too had been torpedoed, there was a large patch of dark oil on the water and wreckage covering about two miles.

We were landed by tender at a little fishing village on the west coast of Scotland and we stayed there for two days. Our adventure had lasted for a fortnight, an adventure we would never forget. We were very grateful to so many people for helping us. The aircraft that came to our aid, the ships and also to the U-boat captain, who had spared our lives. We went home to Cambridge and took with us a compass from the lifeboat and my brother's lifejacket and, of course, so many dramatic memories.

Geoffrey became a Cambridge don and later lived in Hampshire with his wife and two children. Geoffrey told me the story several years ago. I am grateful to his wife, Connie, who allowed me to use his diary, which has enabled us to share his amazing story.

Chapter 19

Christine – 10 years old: Nottingham, England

I was nearly 10 when war began and at that time I was living in Nottingham with my mother and father and my younger sister. In 1939 I was aware that the adults were always talking about the possibility of war. I could read the newspapers so knew that Herr Hitler was making speeches to the German people. I also knew that German soldiers had marched into Austria and were greeted by cheering people. Everyone in Germany seemed to like Hitler.

Where we lived, people were erecting Anderson shelters in their gardens. Some people though, had Morrison shelters in their houses, these looked like large tables which people went underneath for safety. Large Barrage Balloons appeared in the sky. These were raised to a great height and when this happened, the air raid sirens sounded – a loud wailing sound, which frightened me. Both children and adults were issued with gas masks, which we had to put on daily, to ensure that there were no leaks.

My father had joined the Territorial Army two years before war was declared but, after Christmas in 1939, he joined the regular army. He went away for training and did not come home very often, however he had a long leave in 1940, before joining a regiment. My mother went away from time to time to visit him, and my grandmother came to look after us. I always looked forward to her visits. About this time my father became friendly with some American songwriters called Kennedy and Carr, they suggested that I should go to America for safety. I really did not want to do that and, fortunately, my mother was on my side, so that idea was soon forgotten.

I was not evacuated officially, although my mother was very worried that we were in an area that was likely to be bombed. So we packed up and went to a little village outside Nottingham called Clifton and stayed with a retired farmer and his wife. After a week, my mother left us with them and returned to Nottingham, where she had a wartime job working for the Civil Defence. These people were very kind to us and we settled down quickly. We attended the village school, where the children were friendly and made us feel welcome. It really was a delightful village and a very good place to be. It even had a Maypole on the village green!

I went to church on Sundays with the farmer and his wife. He was the churchwarden and, after the service, we went to Clifton Hall where the adults had sherry and the children were given orange squash. I went outside with the other children to play games and climb trees and had a wonderful time.

I really enjoyed living there and I joined the local Brownie pack. We always had a good time and we met weekly in a loft over the local laundry. My mother visited whenever she could and would stay with us at the farm.

After a term we went back to my mother. She had managed to find us a house in a safer district and I went to the local school for two terms. It was there that I sat for the scholarship exam, which I was very lucky to pass. This meant I could go to the local Grammar School. As far as our safety was concerned, we had an Anderson shelter in the garden, but it was on sloping ground so it was not very satisfactory. We had a basement and my mother had the stairs reinforced so that she could work down there, as she still worked for the civil defence. If we heard the sirens we would just go below. This happened regularly and, on one occasion, we heard a great deal of noise, bangs, clattering and a loud tinkling sound. We found later that bombs and shrapnel had fallen onto a disused brickyard and a gun factory in Nottingham. We just hoped and prayed that we would not be hit. If the 'all clear' did not sound until after 3am, we did not have to go to school until after lunch. That always seemed to be quite a treat. We were very lucky not to have much bomb damage where we lived. However, we seemed to be under the path of bombers going to other targets.

At the beginning of 1942, my father was sent to Singapore and at the end of that year, we received a letter from the War Office telling us that he had been taken prisoner. We waited patiently for his postcards, but these did not come very often. Prisoners were allowed to send a postcard with twenty-five words on it written in capital letters. My mother found it all very difficult, she missed my father so much and had almost no news. She spent a lot of time trying to find out where he was and if he was still alive. Every day we watched and waited for a letter to come and we listened to the radio, hoping to get some news. She found out later that he had been transported from Changi jail, either to Balale or the Solomon Islands. We subsequently heard the terrible news that all prisoners who had managed to survive had been shot by the Japanese guards. I could not believe we would never see him again. I think by the time we received his last card, he was already dead. When my mother heard this she was distraught and never really recovered, we all felt lost and so desperately sad.

Our life had to go on even though it was difficult to concentrate on anything. We were very lucky that we had a garden large enough to grow fruit and vegetables and keep chickens. My mother would barter any surplus food for things we were short of; I cannot remember every being really hungry. We used to preserve eggs for the winter and my mother made jam and bottled fruit, some of which was sold at the WI. We also picked blackberries and gathered rose hips; nothing was ever wasted.

My grandmother was very good at dressmaking; she had a large suitcase full of material and would make clothes for us. She and my mother would unravel jumpers, wash the wool, and then knit something else. I think they were very creative.

On VE day I celebrated with a gang of children from school. We went into Nottingham centre and joined in with the singing and dancing and had great fun. We ended up in the local youth club where they had an enormous bonfire and a fantastic party.

When we heard the news that the first Atomic bomb had been dropped and that the war would soon be over, we cheered and were happy, but then I noticed the girl in the next bed was crying. She told us that her brother was a prisoner in Japan and she was worried in case he had been killed. We felt very sorry for her and comforted her the best we could.

On VJ day I was working at a farming camp. We were allowed time off from school to help with the potato picking and sugar beet harvest. Some of the farmers were not very pleasant and wanted free labour, but some did pay us.

We all went into Leicester for VJ night. We were warned that we should stay together as we really shouldn't have been out unchaperoned. We had a very happy evening, lots of laughter, singing and dancing with people we had never seen before, coming up to give us a hug or even a kiss.

The war left me with a dilemma, for many years I felt uncomfortable with Japanese people. We had a Japanese family living quite close to us in Purley, I always wondered if our Japanese neighbour had come into contact with my father. It took me some time for this feeling to disappear. Eventually, we became good friends with the family and we even talked about my father, they were so sorry about what had happened to him.

Christine became a magistrate and now lives in Wiltshire, her family lives nearby.

Chapter 20

John – 6 years old: Ashwell, Herts, England

When war was declared in 1939, I was living with my sister and parents on the outskirts of Ashwell, a village in Hertfordshire. My father worked on the land, so he did not go away to war. It was a village that suffered very little physical damage, most of the young men went away to war, some returned injured physically, some mentally, and some never returned to their loved ones. Men left to join one of the three services. Those left behind helped by working on farms, in factories, the fire service and any other activity involved with war work.

It was a village fairly close to Bassingbourne, an operational RAF station. When war was declared on 3 September, we sat as a family and listened to Prime Minister Neville Chamberlain broadcasting to the nation: 'We are at war with Germany'. The very next day we heard the wailing of air raid sirens, this was the first practice but it was a sound that was to be heard many times after that.

Before long, children from London arrived at the village. A week or two before they arrived, a lady visited every house asking if people would look after an evacuee. My mother agreed to take two children. When they arrived these children were inspected by the local doctor and nurse to see if they were healthy or had nits.

We went with my mother to the village hall to collect our evacuees. The children were sitting at the end of the room, each one had a small case and a gas mask in a cardboard box. They all looked frightened and worried. We were allocated two boys, Jim and Tom. They seemed quite nervous. Our house was very full, but my mother said we all had to help the war effort, our job as children was to share our toys with our new housemates and I had to share my bedroom with my sister. We went home and my mother showed them to their room and went downstairs to make our lunch. Before long, we were all at the kitchen table, the boys were chattering and telling us about their journey from London. They were brothers and they had never seen the countryside before. They were amazed to see animals in fields.

Most of the evacuees had never been out of London before and the coun-tryside must have seemed like another world. Some had never seen cows or sheep or a haystack. A few got up to mischief and were found jumping on the hay, stealing apples and frightening chickens and ducks. Villagers were not at all pleased. The boys we had staying with us were polite and fairly well behaved. They settled down quickly and every day we went to school together.

At that time, RAF Bassingbourne was being constructed. It was a time of enormous activity with lorries, tractors and steamrollers passing through the village. A great number of local men were involved with the building work. The labour went on both day and night. Often the two boys would go up to the fence of the camp and watch what was going on.

One day, we saw a glow in the sky and were told that the London docks were burning. Some people climbed trees to get a better look. The boys were always worried in case their parents were hurt. To help dispel their anxieties, my mother made sure they wrote home every week, they received few letters and they told us their father had joined the army and gone away to war some time before, they never received a letter from him.

One day, I was very surprised to see that our village name sign, on the approach to the village, had disappeared, also the finger posts pointing towards other villages and towns. Even the sign outside the village post office was painted out. The post office just became 'Village Post Office'.

Our school started to have school dinners. Up until this time, children always went home for their midday meal. This was intended to help the working mothers, so that they could stay at their place of work from early morning to late afternoon, at least. The meals were not brilliant, but I think they were nutritious. It was usually a stew-like meal with potatoes and vegetables followed by a tart or milk pudding. It was about this time that we were also given a little bottle of milk to drink, every day.

Quite a few Wellington bombers were lost at the beginning of the war and some bombs were mistakenly dropped by pilots who mistook their positions. One German pilot landed at RAF Steeple Marsden, a satellite station a few miles away. He and his crew got out of their plane and just gave themselves up to an airman, who took them prisoner and then transported them to the Officers' Mess for lunch.

One day a Junkers 88 actually crashed mid-air into a Wellington, the Wellington crashed into a barley field and burst into flames. The Junkers came down on the other side of the village of Ashwell. No one was allowed to approach the village until the crew were found. They eventually found the bodies of the two German pilots. One was wearing an Iron Cross.

The two boys we had staying with us were always searching for souvenirs. The following day we had a visit from the police. They questioned the boys and in their bedroom they found a box full of live ammunition, which they took away. They gave the boys a lecture about the danger of collecting live ammunition!

One night some bombs landed on the village, but nobody was hurt and there was very little damage, however they left several large craters and smashed a sewer pipe.

Everyone who had a garden grew fruit and vegetables, we dug up our rose garden and planted fruit bushes. If people didn't have a garden they had an allotment on land that used to be the recreational playground. Most people worked hard and had more produce than they needed, this was used to barter for other food or sometimes it was sold by the Women's Institute, who made jam and marmalade. My mother made jam from the fruit we grew. Sometimes we went out and collected blackberries, hazelnuts and walnuts .We were allowed extra sugar for jam making and a neighbour of ours was given sugar to feed his bees in the winter. Honey was regularly used to sweeten food and the bees were vital for pollinating the crops.

At school, we collected clean newspapers for recycling and the local dustmen collected them every week. This was to help the 'war effort'. The Girl Guides set out to collect a mile of pennies and this was to support the 'Spitfire' fund. At one time there was a request for metal. All iron railings or metal gates disappeared from gardens and parks and my father even gave away most of our saucepans. All this was collected and stored in the grounds of Merchant Taylors' School in Ashwell.

Our family life went on as before, going to school every day and with my mother looking after the home with four young children. We could hear the planes taking off and returning both day and night, and we saw young men in uniform, occasionally walking around the village and going into the local pub. These young men always seemed to be smiling and laughing. The evacuees fitted in well and made friends with the local children.

Shopping was a long and tedious process involving lengthy queuing. All essential produce required a ration card. Housewives had to plan their menus very carefully so that no food was ever wasted at a meal.

I think my life was very similar to that of other children living in the many villages in England. When the end of the war came we celebrated with street parties, my mother made sandwiches and baked a cake, I think everybody produced food from somewhere. We had a wonderful day, everyone was so happy and relaxed and we didn't go to bed until midnight. People brought out old gramophones and all the adults were singing and dancing.

We were very sad when our evacuees returned to London, as they had become part of our family. We have always kept in touch with them and when my mother died they came to her funeral.

John is a widower who lives on the south coast of England. He worked and owned a small farm in Hertfordshire.

Chapter 21

Birgitta – 12 years old: Sarpsborg, Sweden

In 1939 when the war in Europe began, I lived with my mother and father in the little town of Sarpsborg in Norway. My parents were Swedish but I was born in Norway, so I had dual nationality. We always listened to the BBC news as well as news from Norway and Sweden and had a daily newspaper, so we were aware of the grave situation in the rest of Europe. We went to the cinema, where we saw newsreels of the German Army advancing through the countries of Europe, they seemed to be unbeatable and very powerful. When we heard about the retreat of the British Army at Dunkirk, my father thought that before long, the whole of Europe would be under German domination. We knew that Vidrun Quisling, the Norwegian President, was cooperating with the Germans. My parents did not agree with this and thought he was a traitor. We were relieved when we heard that the Norwegian royal family had escaped to the safety of England.

Norway was occupied by the Germans in April 1940 and before long, we saw German soldiers on our streets. They always looked very smart and confident and I tried to avoid contact with them, to me they were the enemy and they shouldn't be in our country. Some people agreed with the Quisling government and we knew that we had to be careful what we said and to whom we talked. We heard that some people had been arrested for criticising the government.

One morning in June 1940, the police came to the house, accompanied by two German soldiers and asked to see our papers. They said we must report to the police station every week because we were not Norwegian citizens. That night, my parents decided that, as Swedish citizens, we would be safer back home in Sweden. At least there would not be any German soldiers there. They agreed we should wait until the beginning of the school holidays, then no one would realise that we were leaving forever.

We decided to visit our grandparents in a little Swedish town called Tildan, my father said that we must not tell anyone what we were planning to do. He was working as a fireman and we lived in a house next door to the fire station. In order to go to Sweden we needed papers giving us permission to travel. He told the authorities we had to attend a family funeral and fortunately we were given our travel documents. We were constantly anxious about who we could trust, so even our neighbours were told nothing. If anyone saw us leaving, we would say we were going to a family funeral and would be away for a few days.

When we arrived at the railway station, we saw two German soldiers looking at people's papers and checking identities. They looked at ours and waved us through. I was frightened they might ask us to open up our cases and then they would see family photographs and my mother's jewellery. A few weeks later the border between Norway and Sweden was closed.

The train stopped at the border and Swedish border guards came on board and asked to see our papers, they asked why we were going to Sweden. My father told them we were on family business and luckily, we had no trouble getting through. When an official saw we had Swedish passports he wished us luck and asked my father about life in Norway.

I was surprised how relaxed life appeared in Sweden. People standing on pavements chatting to friends and some were actually laughing. In Norway people just hurried about their business, groups of people standing together were banned by German law. I had become very frightened of the German presence, we had heard so many stories about people being taken away for questioning and being deported.

My grandfather managed to find us a small house. Our relatives and their friends gave us furniture, pots and pans, and everything we needed to make a home. Everyone was so kind and generous. It was so good to see all my Swedish cousins again and I soon felt more relaxed and at home, though I missed our house in Norway and my school friends.

My father joined the Swedish Army, which was calling for volunteers. Although Sweden had been neutral for nearly 200 years, it was necessary to have a strong army to patrol our borders. It was an easy way for him to earn money and, as we were neutral, it was not considered a dangerous occupation.

After the summer holidays I started at the local school. The children were very friendly and I soon settled down and became part of the class. For the first two or three weeks I often answered questions in Norwegian, much to the amusement of the other children. There were twins in the class who were refugees from Finland, they also integrated well and even stayed with their foster parents after the war.

Although we were neutral and we did not see German soldiers, we still knew there was war in Europe. We had ration books and even needed coupons to buy clothes. Everything was very expensive and there were many shortages. Coffee was very difficult to obtain and my mother mixed other things with it to make it go further. Before the war, Sweden imported coffee from South America, but now ships were unable to transport supplies. We grew vegetables and kept chickens and bees. I know we received extra sugar to give to the bees in winter. I do not think we were hungry, but there was little variety in the food we ate.

My mother worked for the Red Cross and helped to make up food parcels to send to Norway. She told me they put in dried food, biscuits, tinned goods and even soap. They were never quite sure what they would have to put in, but knew everything was gratefully received.

We were told to put black curtains at all our windows and to ensure that not one chink of light could be seen from outside. We were not even allowed to have lights on our bicycles. I could not understand who was going to drop bombs on us, but I was told we had to obey the rules for our own safety. I discovered later that there was potential for German or British planes to stray over Sweden and drop bombs accidentally, having mistaken their position.

We started to see groups of young men standing around. Apparently they were Norwegians who had escaped over the border from the Germans. Local people gave help and they just seemed to integrate into the community. My uncle once told me he had been to a party in Malmo and had met some RAF pilots who had escaped from Germany. He said they would soon be on their way back to England. Many soldiers and airmen escaped through Sweden.

The Swedish-Norwegian border is very long and impossible to patrol successfully. Quite a few Norwegian resistance workers and some Jewish families also escaped across the border. They were very brave and some were shot trying to escape. We were always amazed when we heard stories of their exploits. Some were so daring. One lady swam in the Oslo fiord and placed explosives on several German ships. She caused a great deal of damage and then had to flee from the Germans. Fortunately, local people helped her to escape to Sweden, although the Germans offered a large reward for her capture. Her story became a legend. Sometimes an advertisement would appear in a local newspaper warning of dire consequences if anyone helped people to escape. Nobody took any notice of this.

Occasionally, my father came home on leave and he would bring a leg of pork or some other treat. He would have been given this by the farmers he had met. For a long time he was stationed with the army on the Finnish border. My mother was always happy when he arrived home and so sad when he left, even though she knew he was never in any real danger.

I think we were really lucky to have lived in a neutral country. We could move around freely and were not worried about being arrested and sent to Germany to work in factories. We did not have German soldiers marching around and watching our every move. There were lots of things we could not buy, but everyone was in the same position. When Germany was finally defeated and peace came to Europe, we returned to Norway to visit family and friends. It was then that we discovered that my uncle and a friend had been shot and killed trying to escape to Sweden, after some act of sabotage. We all felt so sad, but thankfully my aunt and cousins were safe and well.

It took some time for life to get back to normal and we had to get used to the idea that my father was living at home again. Eventually, the shops were able to sell the goods we had been unable to buy during the last five years. When my father left the army, he went back to being a fireman at the local fire station. This time however, it was in Sweden.

Birgitta is married, lives in Alicante, Spain and has a daughter and two grandchildren. When the war ended she trained as a nurse.

Chapter 22

Ray – 2 years old: Hull, England

I was 2 years old when war was declared and I lived with my mother, father and two sisters in Hull. I was the youngest of ten children. Three of my brothers and a sister went away to war. The rest of my family lived locally. My father had been a lieutenant in the King's Own Yorkshire Light Infantry in the First World War and was badly injured in a mustard attack. We lived in a two-bedroom house with a large attic, which was where my two sisters and I slept.

I remember being in bed and hearing the wailing sound of the air raid siren. This always frightened me. Then I would hear my mother telling my sisters to fetch me, wrap me in a blanket and take me downstairs. They put me in the pram, which was by the front door and then they loaded everything on top of me, blankets, kettle, primus stove, bread and jam! My little cat, Soot, came with us in a cardboard box. We quickly made our way to a local warehouse where we sheltered in the basement. There were street shelters nearer but these were dreadful places, smelling of dog dirt, in addition to many other unpleasant smells. Although the basement was cold and damp, I think we felt safe there. An old man, who always came to the shelter, brought with him an old gramophone and lots of records. The people there, including my mother, enjoyed singing along with the music. This helped people to forget the ever-present danger.

Once we were in the shelter, my little cat would curl up and go to sleep. We could always hear the bombs dropping, there seemed to be a terrible scream and then the explosions. Sometimes these seemed to lift up the floor. There was a great deal of noise in the shelter. Some of the ladies were crying and screaming and this made the children even more frightened and they cried too. We were told that the really loud bangs were either 500lb or 1000lb bombs, or land mines. These came down on parachutes and exploded well above the ground, causing so much damage they could flatten a whole street.

Occasionally, the old man would put a radio on and so we would listen to 'Lord Haw Haw', the traitor, broadcasting from Germany, announcing the terrible things that would happen to Britain and particularly to Hull!

He even specified particular buildings, such as the five chimneys on the power station, saying they would not be there in the morning. They were!

When we heard ack ack guns firing at the German planes, everyone cheered and was happy to know that we were fighting back. Often when we came out of the basement, we would be told that some streets were closed due to bomb damage or an unexploded bomb. We then saw the bomb disposal unit arrive to defuse the bomb. There was devastation everywhere. Hull was very badly bombed, but the raids were not reported on the BBC, except to say there had been a raid on 'a north east town'.

As the war progressed, we went to the basement and began to settle down for the night, before the sirens had even sounded. My mother thought this was better than waking me up and rushing us to safety, it also meant that we did not have such a disturbed night.

My father worked as a fire watcher. Every night after work, he would camp out on the factory roof to watch for fires and then alert the fire brigade. He worked at the 'Rainer and Porter' paint factory. Sometimes my sisters and I took him a flask of tea and sandwiches, as he would be positioned there for a long time. He was always pleased to see us.

My mother coped well with feeding the family. She cooked two dishes regularly: meat and vegetable pie, and stew and dumplings. She tried to get a piece of meat to roast at the weekend and would ask for some more fat, which she turned into dripping. This was used on bread or toast for our breakfast, instead of butter. She didn't complain about the rations and we were never hungry, although there was little variety in our diet. Most weeks we had similar food. The only time we had breakfast together was on Sunday morning when we had kippers or an omelette made with powdered egg.

On my birthday in 1941 I was given a blue and red pedal car. It was the best present I had ever had and I was so proud of it. That evening, we went to the warehouse and settled down, as usual, for the night. Suddenly, we woke up and were aware that a huge air raid was taking place. We heard the droning of the planes and we could hear bombs dropping. There was a terrible thump and the floor shook several times and plaster came down from the ceiling. It was so cold and people were moaning or praying. Then suddenly, it was quiet and the raid was over. We went out into the morning light and made our way slowly home.

When we turned the corner to go into our street, my sister just screamed and we stopped and stared. Where our house had been, there was just was a pile of rubble and there was a smouldering heap of ruins all down the street. The houses had either gone or were very badly damaged. We just stayed there crying and could see some firemen were on their knees trying to find out if anyone was under the rubble. It was a sight I will never forget. We discovered that the houses not damaged by conventional bombs, had been destroyed by incendiary bombs. My mother retrieved a little enamel tin with blue around the edges and three unbroken fresh eggs in it! We thought that must have been a miracle. I saw the remains of my little car and felt very sad. What I do remember was the dreadful, sooty smell. Something I was to experience, many times in the future, after a raid.

We were taken to a recovery centre run by the WVS and given a cup of tea and some food. They provided us with temporary accommodation, where lots of beds had been laid out in a long line. We were so grateful to have a place of shelter. We shared our temporary home with many other families.

The next day we went to stay with my grandparents until we could find another house. We had lost everything and, most precious of all, our family photographs. This upset everyone and particularly my mother, who felt that we no longer had any record of our past. She was so sad that my brothers' letters had been destroyed. The next few days were spent looking for anything we could salvage, but I was not allowed to help as they thought it was far too dangerous. We were told that a large landmine had caused the damage. All we could be grateful for was that we were not in the house when it happened. Fortunately, my father found one of my mother's bags, which contained the family's ID cards. He also found half of a silver cup my brother had won at school. It was a horrible feeling to have lost everything.

My mother was keen to keep up with our usual daily routines and insisted that we used the 'bath van' which came to the end of the street. This was a large vehicle divided up into cubicles, in each was a small bath or washbasin. I hated it, but my mother insisted that we kept clean. We were given hard towels, hot water and carbolic soap. This had a horrible smell and we were allowed to keep any we had not used. The towels were very rough!

We then managed to find another house and were given furniture, some new, some second hand. My mother did not like it, but at least we had somewhere to live. We were not there very long when we were bombed out again and once more, everything we had was gone. Three other houses were flattened by a very large bomb that had landed at the end of the street and, as the houses were all attached, the block was razed to the ground. We were homeless yet again but managed to salvage one or two things, including my brother's silver cup. We were now going to the shelter every night and sleeping there.

The area we lived in was continually being bombed and my parents finally thought it would be safer for my sisters and me to be evacuated to the country. As I was so young, it was necessary for at least one of my sisters to be accommodated with me in the same family unit. It was agreed that we should go to the village of Malton in the North Riding of Yorkshire. We met in a large hall on Anlaby Road where we sat with all the other children on long, wooden benches. We were given a label and some string and one of my sisters wrote my name and address on it and tied it to my jacket. My mother had left my elder sister in charge of me. I was frightened and some children were crying. We were given slices of bread and black treacle. I had to carry my gas mask and a small paper carrier bag, which contained my clean clothes; my sisters had their clothes in little cases.

We climbed onto a bus and our long journey began. It was very exciting and it became an adventure. I had never seen fields, sheep or cows before and even the houses looked different. At last we arrived in Malton and were met by a quiet lady, who took us to her house. It was very clean and tidy and there was a blazing fire in the grate. I was given my own bedroom. I looked outside and could see swings and a roundabout in a children's playground. I could hear my sisters talking and laughing. They seemed much happier than I was. I just wanted to be back with my mother, I felt so homesick.

The garden at the back of the house was a beautiful place with grass, trees, flowers and vegetables growing. I ate, what I later found out, was a raspberry. It was all new to me and quite magical, but in spite of this, I just wanted to go home. The next day I planned my escape. The lady had planned to go out to a meeting and told my sisters that they were in charge. When they were not looking, I crept out with my paper bag and walked to the bus stop. A bus stopped and I got on. The conductress asked me where I was going and I just said I wanted to go home to my mum. After helping me off the bus, we went to a nearby chemist's shop, where they decided that I must be an evacuee. On returning to the house later, the lady stated that she no longer wanted the responsibility of me anymore and I should depart immediately back into the care of my parents. She felt too anxious that I might try to escape again. One of my older sisters and her husband came for me in a car. They gave me lunch before travelling home, leaving my two sisters behind. I slept all the way.

My parents were soon rehoused in Maybury Road, on the outskirts of the city. It was an amazingly large house, three stories high with a garden, a garage, and a bathroom. There were thick carpets everywhere. By now, my sisters had returned home. About this time, my mother announced that the butcher was selling horse meat and whale meat. We were not happy about this, but I am sure she used these products and disguised them well!

The air raids continued to be a nightly occurrence. Every night at 6pm, a farmer with his tractor and a trailer drove to the end of our street and took anyone who wanted to go with him. We went to his farm and slept in one of the many barns. The farmer's wife was very kind and provided us with cups of tea, milk, toast and a boiled egg for the children. This went on for nearly a year and then we were offered a permanent home where we stayed for four years. The house we were given had four bedrooms, a bathroom and a toilet downstairs. We were so pleased to have a bathroom, which was considered a great luxury. We also had a garden with an Anderson shelter so no more communal shelters thank goodness.

Opposite our new house was East Park, a fantastic place with a boating lake where I could fish. I spent many hours catching tiddlers and little eels. One of my friend's family had a milk round. Each day, the son put a churn on a handcart and delivered milk, using a ladle to pour the milk into jugs provided by his customers. My friend took the money and I marked the milk ration card. I became good friends with the family and they often let me borrow a bicycle. The same cart was also used to collect shrapnel, bits of incendiary bombs and even silver paper. We took this to a scrap man, who gave us a little money for our efforts. We also gathered glass bottles and jars and later on we collected wool. All this gave us some spending money.

At this time children were expected to go to school at 5 years old. So far, I had avoided going and, by moving from place to place, there was no record of me. My father decided that I must go to school and I knew then there was no argument. I was reluctant to go and tried to fight the system, but in the end I gave up. Once I found that I could read, write, and understand basic mathematics, I began to enjoy my time there.

When I was attending Lincoln Street School, I discovered the 'hot cake shop'. This was a small shop, close to the school, which had a very big brass bell that jingled when you opened the door. The shop had the wonderful smell of freshly baked bread. The owners made sure that there were enough small cakes and buns for all the children to buy. If you paid a penny, they would scrape a little margarine onto them. If you couldn't finish eating it before school began, you just put it in your pocket and ate it bit by bit in the classroom, taking care that the teacher didn't see you. I was never sure if the teacher knew what we were doing. This hot cake was breakfast for many children.

While out exploring, we found an avenue of bombed houses that were boarded up, but the back gardens were full of apple and pear trees. There were also lots of wild raspberries and strawberries growing. We often collected a basket of fruit and took it home. My mother then made delicious puddings for us.

Once in 1943, my two sisters took me to see Disney cartoons, which were showing at the Savoy cinema. It was in the summer and we had 'double summer time' so it was light in the evenings until quite late. We went to the first showing at 6pm and, half way through the film, it came to a halt. The manager came on stage to say that an air raid was taking place, we could either wait and see the rest of the film or go out to a shelter. My sisters decided that we should leave and we started to walk home as there were no buses running. A soldier and a sailor walked past. Suddenly, one of them grabbed us and pushed us over the wall of the Methodist Hall. They made us lie very close to it for protection. Within seconds, we heard bombs whistling down, causing a great thumping sound, together with lots of smaller explosions. My ears really hurt with all the loud noises. Eventually, when it was all quiet, one of my sisters stood up and screamed. I stood up and, to my horror, saw a badly injured horse lying nearby, still with its reins attached to a cart. As there were no buses running, the soldier made sure we knew our way home and wished us luck. It was nearly 11pm when we arrived at the house and my mother was relieved to see us safely back.

One day in 1944, we found that an area close to our school was being used to train soldiers. Later, we realised that this was training for D-Day. There were tanks, jeeps, Bren guns and soldiers everywhere. The soldiers were using blanks and mock grenades, which gave out red and yellow smoke. There was so much noise, but it was very exciting.

When the war ended I was nearly 8 years old, but I had experienced so many different things and, as a family, we had all survived. We just had to wait for my brothers and sister to come home. On VE day we had a party at school and then another in our street. Red and white bunting was put up. Long tables appeared and these were laden with food. We had a huge bonfire, about 30ft high, made from much of the spare wood that was lying around. We even had fireworks!

The streetlights came on again, cars drove with headlights and cinemas stayed open. A few months later, my brothers came home and once again our house was crowded and I had to return to sleep in my room downstairs. This did not matter because everyone was so happy that the war was over.

Unfortunately, my grandparents did not survive. They had been bombed out in 1943 and so went to stay with one of their children. They died soon after that; my grandmother first, and then my grandfather a few months later. My father always blamed the Germans and the bombing for their deaths.

Ray now lives with his wife in Hampshire. He left school at 14 and eventually went to Oxford. He became a barrister and has lived and worked in many different parts of the world.

Chapter 23

Kris – 4 years old: Berlin, Germany

The war for Kris continued with the occupation of Germany by the Allied powers:

I was born in 1935 and was 4 years old when war was declared. I lived in Berlin with my elder brother and my father and mother. All through the 1930s Germany was being taken over by the Nazi party. In those days, Hitler and his party were doing good things for the morale of the German people. Autobahns were being built and Hitler had reclaimed the Sudetenland and Austria and there was a general feeling of well-being. Even the newspapers seemed to support the party.

My mother was aware that war was possible however, and she kept telling my brother that these were terrible times. We did not understand her anxieties and hated seeing her so upset. The newspapers reported the visits of Neville Chamberlain, but he was portrayed as a comical figure, always walking around holding an umbrella! He made three visits to Germany. He and the French Foreign Minister agreed that Germany could retrieve former German territory in Czechoslovakia. As long as they did not take their troops into Poland, Great Britain would take no action. Hitler thought that as he had such a powerful army and air force neither Great Britain nor France would challenge him if he entered Poland.

My father was a judge in Berlin and my parents often invited their friends for dinner. We were sent to bed early, but my brother and I sat outside the dining room door and listened to what was going on. We could hear them laughing and joking about Hitler! They had many Jewish friends. Fortunately, my father knew that certain groups of people were being targeted by the Nazis, so he advised them to leave Germany and to go to the USA or England, as soon as they could. My godfather Otto Furstner was one of these. He published the works of Richard Strauss, Hans Pfitzer, Paul Hinderuth and many others. Some Jews had lapsed in their faith and been baptized as Christians, but since they were born to Jewish parents, the Nazis considered them to be Jewish. My godfather left for England in 1935 and lived there until his death in 1958.

My father was too old to go to war. He was born in 1886, but my mother was much younger and was only 23 when I was born. Many of my mother's family were sent to war. My father spent the war years working in Berlin as a judge.

I started school in 1941 when I was 6 years old. At the beginning, we were taught Gothic script in our handwriting lessons. For most ceremonies and assemblies, we were expected to raise our right arms as a symbol of respect and acknowledgement of authority. This was very tiring, so I used my left arm for support. I was too young to realise the true significance of this salute.

My parents never discussed events like the annexation of Austria or the Sudetenland or any other political incidents. However, I often remember my father pacing to and fro, listening to a wireless that was held close to his ear and we had to keep quiet. He was listening to the BBC. This, of course, was forbidden. My parents told us that we should never tell anyone that my father listened regularly to the wireless. We were also told that if other people knew, we would all be in great trouble.

In the middle of 1941, the air raids on Berlin became more frequent and we were often awakened during the night. We went to a cellar which was used as a communal shelter. At the time we were living in an apartment with twelve flats. We had to cross a street in order to get into the cellar. This was where all the tenants gathered. I remember one time crossing the street and being very frightened because the houses all around were burning. We were so lucky that our block was never hit. We stayed in the cellar until the 'All Clear' sounded and it was safe to return home.

A little while later, the government decided that, wherever possible, women and children should leave Berlin and go to the safety of the country. My mother and a friend decided that we should go to a small village to the east of the River Oder, an area which was then German, but is now Polish. We lived with the other family, my mother's friend and her two sons. We all went to the local school and as we were the only evacuees there, we were no threat to the local population and they made us very welcome. Food was not a problem. Everyone had a ration card and, as we were living in the country, we could buy or grow fruit and vegetables. Many people also kept chickens and bees.

In February 1943, after the Battle of Stalingrad, the German army suffered a great defeat and my mother realised the war was going badly for Germany. There was now a real risk of Russian occupation, so she decided we should leave our village and move west to a town in Thuringia, called

Mulhausen. She was happy and relieved to go there, as this was also where members of her family lived. She reassured us that the war would soon be over, long before the Russians arrived. She was so wrong!

We went to an aunt's house and, as her husband and sons were away fighting in the army, there was plenty of room for us. We also had cousins and other relatives living close by.

Muhlhausen was a very pretty medieval town, quite insignificant from a military point of view and, as far as the local population was concerned, it suffered no air raids and had little active involvement in the war. However, towards the end of March, we began to appreciate that the situation was rapidly changing. We could hear gunfire in the distance and realised that before long, we would be occupied by an oncoming army. We were informed that it was the Americans who were approaching. Although we knew this already, we were very surprised at the speed at which they travelled. On 1 April we went to bed as usual, but when we woke up the next morning and opened the curtains, we saw American troops actually camping in the street!

There had been no bombs and no shooting. Apparently the German Commander had decided to surrender without fighting, in order to save lives. He felt it was ridiculous to keep on fighting when it was obvious that Germany had lost the war.

The Americans were very friendly and we were curious as to who they were. We gathered around and looked at them with their heavy weapons and vehicles. They appeared to be confident and relaxed and gave us chocolate and chewing gum. We asked them for cigarettes for the grown-ups. The following day, they had moved on and the street was empty once again.

Following the agreement reached at the Potsdam Conference in November 1945, Thuringia became part of the Soviet Occupied Zone of Germany. Life became much more difficult then and we did not have enough to eat. The Russian army had to be fed, as well as the local population. We went into the countryside and collected potatoes and any root vegetables we could find. Sometimes we managed to buy two or three eggs. We paid for these things with jewellery and silver, the currency in use.

After Potsdam, the Russians confiscated our house for the military to use and we moved in with friends. My parents had divorced by 1943 and both were remarried. My stepfather was in the army and had been captured by the British. When he was released from his prison camp, he and my mother started to plan our escape back into West Berlin. He was a lawyer and wanted to return to his practice and to his flat. Moving legally to the West was not an option. My stepfather left and a few days later, my mother also made the trip. We were looked after by our relatives. Before going, my mother made plans for us to follow her. She arranged for us to be driven to Berlin in the back of a lorry, hidden under a pile of blankets. The driver was transporting goods to West Berlin. We thought it would be a great adventure and were not afraid. Fortunately, everything went smoothly and the lorry driver bribed his way through every checkpoint. We arrived in West Berlin safe and sound. When the Russians realised that that so many people were travelling to the western sectors by such methods, they took steps to prevent this mass exodus from the East.

We found that Berlin was very badly damaged with piles of rubble everywhere. Fortunately, the area we lived in had escaped most of the bombing and our house was not badly damaged. We were glad to be reunited with my mother and stepfather and before long we were back at school with a degree of routine in our lives. There was little traffic on the roads, so all the children could play safely in the streets. Reconstruction of the city started straight away and there were men working everywhere. We all had our ration cards, but food was very scarce and we often felt hungry. My parents sold their belongings to buy food.

In 1948 the Soviet Union started the Berlin Blockade, preventing all supplies getting into Berlin and this made life very difficult indeed. The Allied forces, especially the British and the Americans started the 'Berlin Air Lift.' Planes flew in every few minutes, day and night, to keep the city alive. In addition, RAF flying boats brought supplies and landed on the lake in the city. They even brought coal and flour. This continued for a year and, in spite of the Russians, it was a success. It was such a change, as previously we had dreaded the Allied aeroplanes, but now every plane coming to Berlin was welcomed. The people of Berlin will always be grateful. The Deutsche Mark was introduced and the Marshall Plan made recovery possible. Everyone worked very hard and eventually, life in West Berlin returned to normal. However, it was difficult to visit relatives in the East and it remained like this until the Berlin Wall came down in 1989 and Berlin was united once again.

Kris has retired as a barrister and lives in France with his wife. He has three daughters and several grandchildren.

Chapter 24

Eric, Barbara and Ros: Jersey

T he following is a chapter that includes the reports of three children who lived in different parts of Jersey, in the Channel Islands, the only part of the British Isles to be occupied by the invading German army during the Second World War.

Eric – 10 years old: Jersey

I was 10 when the war began and lived on the outskirts of St Helier, where my parents had a small shop. We also owned some fields where flowers, potatoes and tomatoes were grown for export. I was very aware of the impending war as I listened to the wireless and enjoyed reading the newspapers. We read that Hitler was aggressive and had marched his armies into Austria and Czechoslovakia.

Three years earlier, in 1936, one of my cousins had travelled to Berlin to watch the Olympics. On his return, he told us that he had seen Hitler addressing the crowd. He thought that he was a very charismatic and powerful man and the German crowd appeared to idolise him.

On Sunday 3 September, I sat quietly with my parents, listening to the wireless. We heard Mr Chamberlain announce that we were at war with Germany. It did not occur to any of us that a year later we would be occupied by thousands of German troops.

In July 1940 the German Army arrived. The British Government realised that it was impossible to defend this vulnerable island, which was situated only 19 miles off the coast of France. Before the Germans arrived, a plane flew over the island and dropped leaflets stating that we must hang white sheets out of windows, as a sign of surrender. Two days later, we watched with amazement as German aircraft flew over the island before landing at the airfield. There seemed to be so many planes. The Bailiff met the German commander and accepted the conditions for the occupation. The Germans then promptly marched to St Helier, where they lowered our flag and raised the Swastika. It seemed to me that very soon after that, German flags were flying all over the island. They were to fly there for the next five years.

We were very apprehensive about how the Germans would behave and how our daily lives would change. They sang when they marched and always looked very smart. The soldiers went into local shops and bought whatever they needed and even travelled on the local buses. They had been told to be polite and correct when they came into contact with local people. The soldiers paid for the goods they bought with their own 'scrip' for payment. A short while after their arrival, we too were issued with paper money. This was partly due to a shortage of money caused by the soldiers collecting coins as souvenirs.

The Germans immediately imposed many new laws and regulations. Every night I would read the latest ones to my mother while she was preparing our evening meal. These rules also appeared on notice boards. From early on in the occupation, everyone was forced to drive on the right hand side of the road. At first, this was difficult, confusing and somewhat dangerous. A curfew was imposed with dire warnings if it was not observed. Fishing boats were allowed to sail out from one or two harbours, but they needed a permit and usually a German guard would accompany them. When they returned, the Germans would take most of the catch. Some of the beaches remained open and I can remember collecting seawater when we were short of salt. My mother tried boiling potatoes in it but this was not very satisfactory. Most of the beaches however, were mined and had warnings of this posted on notice boards, guards could always be seen patrolling the cliff tops.

At the beginning of the war we could receive the BBC news, but before long, this was banned and all wireless sets were confiscated. Many people ignored this rule and sets were hidden in unlikely places. We listened to the news and wrote it down so that it could be shared with others. There was one special broadcast, early in the morning, which was very helpful because it was given at dictation speed. This was my job and I had to write neatly and take care that we were not discovered undertaking this now illegal daily task. Friends and acquaintances came to the shop and were taken into a back room to read the latest bulletin. We had to be vigilant, just in case German soldiers came into the shop at the same time.

School continued as normal, except that German was taught in secondary schools from the age of 11. At the beginning of the war I attended a little private school, but the teachers were soon evacuated and the school closed. Before the invasion, anyone who had been born in the United Kingdom or was Jewish was advised to leave, but some stayed and were later interned in Germany. This was especially significant for the Jewish families who lived on the island, some remained and were hidden, but many were deported to Auschwitz concentration camp.

From time to time, Allied planes dropped leaflets onto the beaches. These were written in German and were intended as propaganda for German soldiers. When this happened, my friends and I scrambled down the cliffs to retrieve them. We took them to school where my teacher translated them and then they were distributed to local people. This was a very dangerous thing to do, as punishment if caught, was transportation to a concentration camp.

We were careful about to whom we spoke, and what we said in public. Occasionally, someone reported a misdemeanour to the Germans who always acted on the information; unfortunately not everybody could be trusted.

Daily life went on but there were many shortages. There was a lack of fuel for example, so cooking was difficult and, as time went on, the situation deteriorated even more. I was regularly sent out into the countryside to look for anything that we could burn. We had frequent power cuts and my father made small petrol lamps using old tins, but the light from these was dim and it was very difficult trying to complete homework in these conditions, some of our teachers were not sympathetic.

As far as food was concerned we were lucky, we owned fields and grew potatoes, tomatoes, beans, sugar beet and other vegetables. This helped my mother and we sold the surplus in the shop. When the Allied Forces invaded France in 1944, no supplies could get through and people on the island were starving. A Red Cross ship called the SS *Viga* arrived bringing a cargo of precious supplies such as fuel for cooking, salt and soap. The Germans supervised the distribution and, surprisingly, were under orders not to take anything for themselves. By now, they too were very short of food and provisions. Coincidently, there seemed to be more burglaries; we assumed it was either the slave labour or German soldiers who were responsible.

People were allowed to travel around the island, but they had to keep away from military installations and areas that were mined. Jersey is only a small island and there were only a few buses running. People used horse drawn carts or bicycles. We had some horses stabled at our house and my sister rode them regularly. When people were evacuated to England they gave their animals to neighbouring farmers. The horses were put to work on the farms; they were particularly useful as they replaced the machinery that used up precious fuel.

The Germans brought slave labour to the island. Most of these poor men came from Russia, Poland and the Ukraine. They were treated badly and were dressed in rags. They had no proper shoes or boots, just cloth tied round their feet and they were starving. Local people felt sorry for them and many risked punishment by helping them. Some even gave them shelter and food. I remember sitting at the kitchen table with an escaped Russian prisoner. My mother had given him a hot drink and food and hidden him until he was taken to a 'safe house'. If anyone was caught helping these wretched men, they were sent to a camp in Germany. This actually happened to some of our friends. After the war, several people received gold watches from Russia as a thank you for their help.

Most Germans living on the island were friendly and lived in houses which had been vacated by evacuees. They were not usually armed and sometimes gave us lifts to school in their horse drawn carts. It was only the SS and the Nazis who we really feared. They appeared on the island from time to time.

When people heard that the Allies were advancing through Europe, they became very excited and knew that the war was nearly at an end. We listened to every broadcast on the BBC and soon heard that it was VE day. The next day we heard Winston Churchill's speech, declaring that the war was over. Everyone was cheering and shouting. We had our windows open and our wirelesses on very loudly so that anyone passing by could hear. There were no German soldiers to be seen, I think they had all gone back to their barracks and were keeping a low profile.

The following day, landing craft full of soldiers arrived at St Helier. What excitement there was when they landed! They gave the children sweets and adults cigarettes. People were crying and laughing, and everyone seemed to be kissing someone, friends and strangers alike. It was hard to believe that we were at peace, at last. The German flag was lowered and the Union Jack and the Jersey flag were raised once again. A band played the national anthem and other patriotic tunes. This was such an emotional time for all the island people, even the soldiers had tears in their eyes. To this day, island people celebrate Liberation Day. We are determined that this episode in our history will never be forgotten.

The German soldiers became prisoners of war and some stayed behind to clear the mines from the beaches. The slaves were released, fed, given clothing, and were provided with somewhere to recuperate. We were told that our soldiers were surprised to find them in such poor condition. They were eventually repatriated to their own countries.

Barbara – 12 years old: Jersey

It was the end of the summer holidays in 1939, my sisters and I were playing on the veranda when we noticed several ladies crying and talking to my mother.

It was obvious that there was something seriously wrong. My mother came and told us that war had been declared and she was not sure what was going to happen to us as a family. My father was a professional soldier and we had been living in Gibraltar for nearly two years. I had four sisters and a brother.

The next day, my father and all the other soldiers were confined to barracks. He was seldom allowed to come home and only occasionally returned to ensure that we were safe and there were no problems. We went back to school and life continued as before. About nine months later, my father told us that we had to pack everything we could carry because, with all the other women and children, we were going to the UK on a luxury liner. He had to stay behind with his regiment.

We were escorted home by a flotilla of small ships. After five days, as we sailed through the Bay of Biscay, all the alarms sounded and we saw German planes approaching. Everyone was so frightened and people began crying. Fortunately however, the planes did not attack us and we continued our journey without any more incidents. Eventually, we arrived in Liverpool and were asked by an officer where we would like to go. My mother thought we should go to Jersey, as that had once been her home and she had relatives there.

We set off for London and, each morning for the next four days, waited at Waterloo Station for a train to Weymouth. This was quite a challenge for my mother as she had six children to look after and my youngest sister was only 18 months old! Unfortunately, this was the time of Dunkirk and we saw hundreds of injured soldiers coming off the incoming trains. I was very frightened as I watched this spectacle; some of the soldiers were badly injured and had nurses travelling with them. It was a traumatic experience and one that remained in my thoughts for many years. We eventually caught a train to Weymouth and bought boat tickets for Jersey. As we arrived at our destination, we were amazed to see my aunt, uncle and six cousins just about to depart for England. My aunt suggested that we use their house until we were settled. My mother wondered whether we too should return to the UK, but found that there were no more places on boats. So we had to stay. One lady at the harbour commented that an invasion was unlikely and thought that there was mass hysteria on the island.

We travelled to my aunt's house and decided that it would be a good place to stay. We were so relieved to have a home to live in. There was some tinned and dried food left in the cupboards and clothes hanging in the wardrobes. Fortunately, we could use the clothes and other things such as sheets, pots and pans, and towels that had been left behind. We thought we were so lucky and relaxed once more.

At that time the shops on the island were still well stocked, but we were in a poor position as my mother's army allowance had not yet arrived. In addition to our plight, there was no news from my father as he did not know where we were. The Red Cross tracked us down in the end, so eventually his letters found their way to us. My mother was very short of money and found it difficult to make ends meet. After a while, an advocate (Jersey solicitor) told her about the Howard Davies Foundation. We were subsequently awarded a bursary, which provided some money on a weekly basis. This really saved us.

We were always anxious that the Germans would invade the island. At the end of July, several planes flew overhead and attacked some trucks in St Helier that were full of potatoes and tomatoes. Nine people were killed during that raid and many more were badly injured and went to hospital. We heard later that the Germans thought the trucks were full of guns and ammunition. They then dropped sheets of paper throughout the area, with an ultimatum to the islanders. These instructed people to hang out white sheets from their windows as a symbol of surrender. The next day our Bailiff was summoned to the airport to meet the Germans and to receive the surrender conditions. The Bailiff asked everyone to remain calm and to avoid trouble. We went to St Helier and watched our flag being hauled down and the German flag raised. It seemed that German flags were everywhere.

People were told to hand in any guns or shotguns, even though so many farmers needed guns to keep the rabbit population down. My mother found life very difficult without my father. A communal kitchen was set up in the town and we went to get food. My teacher realised that we were always hungry and arranged for me to help in the kitchen. In this way, I was offered any food that was left over at the end of the day.

Every Wednesday evening, I walked to a nearby farm and asked the farmer's wife if she had any spare food. Sometimes she just told me to see if there were any spare potatoes or vegetables in the fields. Anything that was found was made into a delicious stew. Occasionally, we were even given a rabbit, a tasty and nutritious treat. Eventually, we managed to grow some vegetables in the garden and reared chickens and rabbits, this all helped to feed our hungry family.

We were always apprehensive about the Germans, but if you behaved and obeyed their rules, you were generally left alone. On several occasions I saw them marching through St Helier, with a military band playing and rifles on their shoulders. My brother loved the music and the marching, but I hated it. The young soldiers looked so confident, but I just tried to keep out of their way. Some of them were not much older than my 15-year-old brother.

School continued as usual, but from the age of 11, we had to learn German. The Germans gave us all textbooks and checked regularly that we were making progress. One morning, the whole school was marched to a square in St Helier. A German officer told us that if we would like a packet of sweets, we should give the German salute. Of course, everyone gave a smart salute and we were given the sweets. What we did not know was that a photograph of this appeared in German newspapers and even in the Jersey daily paper, saying that the children of Jersey were all happy now that the Germans were here. We really fell for that trick!

One night, I stayed with a friend and, after supper, we went to her bedroom where she lifted a floorboard and took out a crystal set (wireless). She finally tuned it and managed to get some music, which I thought was quite magical. I remember the tune, as if it were yesterday: *When You Wish Upon a Star*. This tune became very special for me. My friend and her family were taking a huge risk having a wireless. Some people had been deported to Germany for just listening to the BBC.

Eventually, we heard that liberation was imminent and there was a feeling of expectation and excitement everywhere. It was wonderful when the British soldiers actually landed on Jersey soil. There was such a very happy atmosphere. We were given sweets and cigarettes and we didn't see any more German soldiers. I even heard a band playing *When You Wish Upon a Star.*

We then had to wait for our relatives to return and to be reunited with my father. Once again we were a proper family and after the war we settled in Jersey.

Ros – 5 years old: Jersey

I lived with my parents and my four siblings. My father was Captain George Snowden and he was in the Royal Naval Reserve. He was a man of strong principles and high moral standards, sometimes even putting his family at risk. He was warned about this by the Bailiff, who came to his aid on more than one occasion.

My father managed to get permission from the Germans to take his boat, the SS *Normand*, over to Granville in France to bring back essential commodities for the island. This he did under the strict understanding that he should carry only 'essential commodities'. He always took a Jersey crew and flew the Jersey flag when out at sea. On one occasion, he realised the Germans were loading guns and ammunition onto his boat. He remonstrated with the German official, whereupon he was taken to the 'high command'. Two officers entered the room and insisted that my father should salute them. He refused. As a Royal Navy Reserve captain and dressed in civilian clothes, he said he could not possibly salute while in civilian clothes and told them that he was senior to them in rank anyway! The exasperated Germans told him that he would be arrested and sent to Germany to be imprisoned. My brother, who was with him on the boat, ran to friends of some standing and they pleaded his case. He was later taken back to Jersey on another boat and the Bailiff fortunately managed to resolve the situation. My father was not allowed to make any more trips to Granville!

On another occasion, he refused to allow the Germans to use a flat we owned. For this he went to prison for sixty days. When he was released, my mother and brother had to carry him home as he was so weak. He did not manage to prevent them from using the flat, so his protest was in vain. Eventually, after a persuasive discussion with the Bailiff, he agreed to stop his 'one man war' with the Germans.

Some incidents had a surprising element to them.

One time, I was playing with my brother in a public paddling pool when a boy threw stones at us, one of which hit me on the head. My head was bleeding and, before we could do anything about it, a young man ran across, picked me up and took me to the chalet in the gardens of Le Petit Chateau de la Mer. I carried on crying because I thought I was being taken away by the Germans. The young man bathed the wound and bandaged my head, then took me home to my parents. He was a German Naval officer and his name was Werner Szablewski. My father wrote a letter thanking him for being so kind and added that if could be of any help in the future to let him know.

After the war had ended, my father received a letter from Werner, who was by now in a PoW. camp in England. He asked if my father could possibly help him to get repatriated quickly, as his wife and child were in the Russian sector, where life was very difficult. My father did manage to help and Werner got home and was able to help his family escape to the West. A few years, later they visited us in Jersey. On that summer afternoon when Werner helped me, nobody would have imagined that one day our families would become really good friends. Even after my father died my mother visited them several times in Germany. We are still in close contact with them.

All these people still live in Jersey and are now retired.

Chapter 25

Adrian – 5 years old: Gosport, England

I was 5½ at the beginning of the war and lived with my father, mother and sister in Gosport on the South Coast of England, close to Portsmouth. My father was a dentist working in the town when war was declared. He was told that he was too old to go to war, but his contribution was to run the school dental clinics. My grandfather, who was a retired dentist, took over the practice and my father and uncle helped with evening clinics as the workload was immense.

At that time, I was not really aware of what was going on. I watched the barrage balloons being raised and lowered and, whenever we heard the air raid siren sound, we went to the shelter in the garden. This was an Anderson shelter which had been dug out and it was a dark, dank, miserable place. My father had put in a wooden floor and bunk beds and we had a large supply of candles for light. This did make it all a little more pleasant. We also took a supply of tea and cake and some board games to keep us occupied.

As time went on, I became more aware of my surroundings and started to notice what was happening. I knew that when the six o'clock news came on, we all had to be quiet or go out of the room. These were the times when I learned how to play 'shove halfpenny' and Canasta.

From early on in the war, the Germans began to bomb Portsmouth which is, as the crow flies, very close to our home. After work my father was involved with fire watching. In 1940, the Germans blitzed Portsmouth and from Gosport the whole sky was a vivid orange, red colour. There was a strong smell of burning coming across the harbour, a smell I will never forget. One time we could smell the burning of paint, we later read in the local paper, that a paint factory had been hit and set on fire.

My father was allowed to keep his little Austin car. He was given a special petrol ration so that he could drive to Southampton to collect oxygen for anaesthetics. It was a great treat for me when I was allowed to go with him on these trips.

At the beginning of the war, Gosport was declared an evacuation area and the evacuation of children started in 1939. About six months into the war, my mother decided that we were living in a very dangerous area. As she did not want my sister and I to be evacuated, we moved to a little tin house (commonly known as a Nissen hut) in Waterlooville. This was only four miles to the north, but she thought we would all be safe there. Very soon it became apparent that the German bombers were using Waterlooville as a turning point after they had bombed Portsmouth. Any bombs still on board were dropped. Two incendiary bombs landed on two houses close to ours and both were badly damaged. My mother quickly decided that we should return to Gosport, where she thought we would be safer and where we would be in our own home with all our belongings.

In those days people either walked, travelled by bus or rode a bicycle. The buses were always full and near the bus station was a café used by the drivers, who went in for large cups of tea and a bun. There was one spoon on the counter which was attached to a lavatory chain to ensure that it was not stolen. The lady behind the counter had a very large metal teapot. Several cups were set out in a line and she just poured out the tea going along the line without stopping, filling the cups but spilling tea all over the counter, much to the amusement of small boys watching.

All the railings around the houses were taken away and melted down to make aeroplane parts. We had railings around our dental surgery. Mr Watson, who worked for the practice, prevented ours from being removed by saying they were necessary to help people coming down the steps after an anaesthetic. It seems amazing that they accepted that excuse, even though it was true. The railings are still there to this day.

Close to the beach, at Stokes Bay, there was a grand old house named Bay House, owned by Colonel Sloane Stanley. In the early days of the war it was requisitioned and the colonel went to live on the Isle of Wight. The roads in the area were sealed off with barbed wire and poles. There were always 'Red Caps' (military police) milling around. They were there to stop anyone getting into the grounds, which later became known as Stanley Park. This was a great challenge to boys! Once in, we had to be very careful not to be seen. If we were caught, no excuse or explanation was accepted. We were escorted out, accompanied by really bad language, words that were new to us, but soon became part of our vocabulary! Somehow we knew we should, on no account, use these words at home in front of our parents.

From July 1940, all the beaches were closed so we could no longer go to Stokes Bay, a very long and popular beach. Browndown Range, near the beach, was commandeered by the Royal Marines.

Although the war had been going on for some time and people accepted that there was a war on, everyone was still very afraid of air raids. On one occasion we could hear activity in the sky high above us. Even though it was very noisy, we could not hear the usual ack–ack guns firing. We soon realised it was a dogfight between the Luftwaffe and the RAF. It was a beautiful clear day and vapour trails criss-crossed the blue sky. People were standing in the street just watching and cheering despite the attempts by the Air Raid Warden to move people into the air raid shelters.

Portsmouth was, by this time, suffering from regular bombing. The daytime raids were brief, but violent. The Germans were targeting the Royal Naval Dockyards and the many naval ships berthed there. Many sailors lived in Gosport and travelled by ferry across the harbour to Portsmouth, a distance of about 500yds. Close to the ferry on the Gosport side, there was an important submarine base, HMS *Dolphin*. Nearby there were facilities for loading depth charges, torpedoes and shells for the ships and submarines.

In August, Gosport suffered a daylight raid where a great deal of damage was inflicted: Thorngate Hall, Market House and the Ritz cinema were totally destroyed by incendiary bombs and the bombing continued for the rest of that year. During this time, many other significant buildings were also destroyed, including the Town Hall and the Post Office. So many other buildings and houses were destroyed or damaged. The Congregational church lost its beautiful stain glass windows.

The noise during these raids was intense and if we were at school, we ran into a brick shelter built in the grounds, taking with us our gas masks. Quite often, after these raids, our parents collected us early from school. On one occasion, the sirens sounded and before long we heard and saw a large formation of German bombers flying northwards, at a very high level. They passed over and the 'All Clear' sounded and we felt safe and relieved that we were not the target. Later, the siren sounded again and we watched the large formation returning. On the wireless that evening, we heard that that Coventry had been heavily bombed that day, so we assumed those planes must have been heading there and back.

My mother always seemed to be calm. She worked hard caring for two children, my father (who came and went at irregular times) and a home. Much of her time was spent queuing for food and helping the WVS. She coped well feeding the family, in spite of rationing and deprivations. She made wonderful potato scones, scrambled eggs and omelettes from dried eggs, these we found to be quite delicious.

Many of the roads around Gosport were closed to the general public; even the main road between Lee on the Solent and Gosport was closed for the duration of the war. If one wanted to go from Lee to Gosport it was necessary to take a detour via The Lanes.

In 1942, The Nova Scotia Highlanders arrived in Gosport and were billeted at Fort Brockhurst. They were very friendly and kind to us children. They had their tanks parked in the various roads about the area and could be found making toast on billy cans. They gave us some of the toast, which to me seemed to be the best toast ever. The local people grew very fond of these friendly soldiers and often gave them cups of tea and invited them into their homes.

The soldiers smoked their own brand of cigarettes called 'Sweet Caporals'. There were pictures of both German and Allied planes on the packets and inside a card illustrating an aeroplane. The idea was that these pictures would help the soldiers recognise enemy aircraft aeroplanes quickly. A great number of children in the area collected these cards and before long they became a commodity with which to barter. I heard that on one occasion, the soldiers made the children queue in an orderly manner before giving out the cards. They then gave each child four cards. Sometime later these men left with a pipe band playing. We never really knew where they went, but later heard on the wireless that a large number of Canadian soldiers had been killed in the disastrous Dieppe raid.

As the war progressed we continued with our adventures in Stanley Park. We needed bamboo canes for our bows and arrows and we found a plentiful supply of excellent cane there. Also, there was a wood where we could climb the trees and watch what was going on in Stokes Bay. We watched the construction of the Mulberry harbours. We were high up in the trees and could see these enormous contraptions, some even had what appeared to be legs. We had no idea what they were. We were unaware that this was the beginning of the preparations for D Day.

Opposite Bay House, was a riding school with large fields, full of trucks, tanks and armoured vehicles. Jellico Avenue and Western Way had special concrete blocks put down and tanks parked there. My mother made tea for the soldiers, who were always pleased to receive any act of kindness. One day, an uncle who was a soldier visited and stayed for a few hours before his departure. Alverstoke and Elson had convoys of tanks and armoured vehicles parked in preparation for a continuous embarkation of landing craft from a ramp at Hardway. This area was out of bounds to everyone, except residents and officials.

Towards the end of the war, the Germans started to send Doodlebugs, which often flew over Gosport. Everyone was greatly relieved when they had passed over. One actually landed in the village of Stubbington, not far from Lee-on-the-Solent. We were shocked at the devastation it had caused when we went to see what had happened.

After D Day, large numbers of German prisoners of war were brought back to England and disembarked at Hardway. These men were marched to a transit site behind St Vincent's barracks. They wore dirty grey uniforms and people just stood silently as they marched by. Some of them looked so young. We heard later that some were only 16 years old. It was hard to believe these soldiers had been among those who had earlier conquered more than half of Europe.

We also heard about one immaculately dressed German Officer. He wore polished jackboots, riding breeches and special gloves. He became difficult and refused to obey orders. He was told to go left, but refused. The guard just hit him on his thigh, using the butt of his rifle, he soon obeyed all subsequent orders. Some of the PoWs were employed putting up fences around Bay House and also supported local building work.

When we heard about VE day, everyone was very happy and relieved. There were parties all over Gosport and Alverstoke. Where I lived, a huge outdoor party was organised, tables were taken outside and people brought food and drink, everyone had a great time. All the boys in the area got together and built a massive bonfire in the nearby Bay Road. We cut down gorse and towed it to our chosen site. We took anything that would burn. There were bonfires alight all over the town. It was wonderful to find roads, which had been closed for nearly five years, were now open and the street lights turned on once more. Our war was finally over.

Adrian became a dentist and lives in Alverstoke with his wife, he has three children and several grandchildren.

Chapter 26

Sara – 9 years old: Czechoslovakia

(This lady asked for her name to be changed)

In 1939, I was living in a small town in Czechoslovakia with my parents, brothers and sisters. My father was a carpenter who owned his own small business. He always seemed to have a lot of work and, consequently, we had a fairly comfortable life.

We were very aware that Europe was in turmoil. Germany had already invaded Austria and part of Czechoslovakia, which they claimed was the Sudetenland and so was believed to be part of Germany. We heard that Jews in Germany and Austria were being harshly treated and that some were leaving Germany and travelling to England or America. We also heard that some Jewish families had been relocated to the East of Germany. When we heard this we believed that they must have upset the authorities in some way. We listened to the wireless and read daily newspapers, so felt we were well informed. As far as we were concerned, we had lived here for four generations and my great grandfather had started a profitable business.

Just before 1939, Czechoslovakia was forced to hand over the area known as Slovakia to Hungary. In our small town, everyone knew one another and my father was in great demand for his skills. We all went to the local school and I had many friends both Christian and Jewish and as far as we knew, we had no problems.

Once Hungary had taken over the area in which we lived however, things changed overnight. New laws were passed and there were few to protect families like ours. My father found that people began to dispute bills they were given, stating that he had over charged them. This had never happened before. There was no one to help; the police were not sympathetic. As a family, we were blond and blue-eyed. We did not look Jewish, nor did we attend the Synagogue regularly. My mother told us that we must not draw attention to ourselves and should go about our usual business. One morning, we went to school and were told by our teacher that all Jewish children should leave the building, go home and not return. It was then that we realised that we must become invisible.

All Jews were obliged to wear a yellow star. The police came to our house, accompanied by a German soldier and told my parents to report to the police station with our papers. Although my mother had been born a Christian, the police decided that we were a Jewish family and therefore obliged to wear the yellow star. They stated that Jews were not permitted to marry Christians, despite my mother protesting that it had not previously been illegal when she married my father in Czechoslovakia. Our family business was then confiscated and given to a non-Jewish man. Suddenly we felt very vulnerable.

Thankfully, my father was offered a job by the new owner. He was not happy about this, but he had to take it so that he could continue to support his family.

One day, I was walking along the street with a friend when we saw two SS officers coming towards us. As we stepped aside off the path, to let them pass, one of them raised a stick and hit my friend very hard across her shoulders and said that in future we must move more quickly. She actually fell to the ground, but nobody helped her, people just continued walking by as if we did not exist. From then on, we were very frightened and whenever we saw German soldiers or Hungarian police, we kept right out of their way. We heard rumours about what was happening to Jews, but we believed that as we had a safe home and friends, we would not be in any danger.

Some of my school friends no longer made contact and if I ever saw Nazi soldiers, I tried to hide. As I was not obviously Jewish, sometimes I did not wear the yellow star. At this time, Hungarians were fighting alongside the Germans on the Eastern Front and were also in Russia. Young Jewish men were not allowed in the army, but were conscripted and sent for labour work. They were told that this was how they could help their country. We later found out that many of them had been secretly deported to the Ukraine and shot by the Nazis.

Our prime minister had refused to have the Jewish population deported or relocated, so we felt fairly safe. Radios were banned and newspapers were expensive, so we relied on friends and relatives for news. Jews were not allowed to travel on trams or trains but, apart from that, life seemed fairly normal. My brother, sisters, and I now went to a Jewish school, but we still missed our old friends.

My mother managed our home and we always had a meal on the table. Some things were in short supply, but she could cook a nutritious vegetable stew and occasionally, we ate rabbit or chicken. We grew fruit and vegetables and had a few chickens, rabbits and some beehives.

In early 1944, the Hungarian Government realised that the Germans were losing the war and sought an armistice with the Allies. Consequently, the Germans invaded Hungary and put a fundamentalist SS officer, Colonel

Adolf Eichmann, in command. He hated Jews and his main aim was to rid Hungary of them all. He ordered us to leave our homes and to move into ghettoes. We were transferred to a small village, just outside the town. My father and I went to the local police station with the deeds of our house and some other important documents, for which we were given a receipt. They told us not to worry, but we were to be relocated to the East and one day, after the war, we could return to our home. When we got back to our house, my mother had filled two large suitcases and began to reassure us that we wouldn't be in danger. She packed jewellery, photos, a change of clothing for everyone, and some bedding.

We went to the ghetto and were allocated a small house, which we had to share with another two families. It was not pleasant and we all slept in one room. My younger sister cried because she had to sleep on the floor. It was just as well we did not realise that this was luxury, compared to what we were about to experience.

One day, we woke up to a great deal of noise. Cars and lorries were being manoeuvred, there was shouting and doors banging. We looked out of our windows and saw the Hungarian police and German soldiers with rifles and dogs, shouting at people to get dressed and packed. A soldier was standing by our door and we just did as we were told. We went out and were pushed towards a lorry and told to climb into the back quickly. We saw one lady being hit on the head by a rifle butt, just because she was slow and struggling. She was old and couldn't move any faster, she fell and nobody could help her. The dogs were barking and there was so much noise. My mother told me to hold onto my sister and on no account to let go. We must keep together she said.

We were driven to the railway station and there, in front of us, was a train with cattle trucks and a line of armed soldiers with dogs. We were shoved and pushed into the trucks and told to move quickly. We were the first family in, so we went to the far side, where we could see some chinks of light. We believed that, at least, we would be able to breathe some fresh air and possibly see the countryside as we travelled. More and more people were herded in and then the doors were slammed shut and we were in the dark. All this time the soldiers were shouting and we could hear dogs barking and every few minutes, we heard gunshots.

I became aware that people were crying and saying prayers; children just clung to their parents. It was suffocating. We were told that we were going to a place in the east called Auschwitz, a labour camp, but nobody knew anything about it. I thought that if it was a labour camp, my father would find work and we could all be together. Occasionally, we had a whiff of fresh air, but if we turned towards the other occupants of the truck, it was just hot, stuffy and incredibly smelly. There was a bucket for a toilet, but nobody could use it. There was no room and no privacy. We were so hungry and thirsty and the food and drink my mother had brought disappeared very quickly.

Eventually, the train stopped and we could see more soldiers through the slats. We could see dogs and men dressed in striped pyjamas and, in the distance, we could see barrack huts. I still believed that this was a labour camp where my father might be able to work. I thought we could still be a family.

When we were in the ghetto, my mother heard stories about people being taken into forests to be shot, then dumped in large graves. The Nazis were clever and used the men in striped pyjamas to get us down from the trucks and to take charge of us. They wanted us to believe everything would be fine. Our family was then just torn apart. My mother and two of my sisters were sent to the right, my father and brother to the left, and my sister and I to another line. We held hands so tightly that we could not be separated. All the time, I could see two soldiers taking photographs and laughing. Everyone else was quiet and frightened. I did not see any member of my family ever again.

We were sent to a large barrack block next to a red brick building, which we discovered later to be a crematorium. On that first day, Rachel and I watched the long columns of people going to the building for what we thought was a shower. We thought it strange that we did not see anyone coming out. That night, my sister and I slept together on a bunk, cuddling to keep warm and for comfort.

Everyone around us looked terrible, so thin and gaunt and all the ladies were wearing dirty, shapeless dresses. The smell in the hut was indescribable. After a few days, we were no longer aware of the smell. The two ladies who had bunks next to ours were friendly and advised us to eat everything we could and also to do anything we were ordered to as quickly as possible. We needed to remain anonymous and never have eye contact with the guards. They told us about the dreadful things that were happening in the camp and said that it was imperative that we keep healthy. Being able to work meant that you might have a chance of survival.

Next morning, we were given some watery soup and a piece of bread to eat. Then we were sent to a large building, where we had to shower and then stand in a line to have our heads shaved. We were given some horrible liquid and told to put it all over our bodies (some form of disinfectant, I assume).

We were issued striped baggy dresses, which we pulled on over our heads. We were sent to a large building to sort out clothes and the contents of suitcases. We worked quickly and the guards left us alone. After a few weeks, we were sent to the Birkenau section of Auschwitz to forced labour. We were escorted to a hut full of machines, with women working hard. We started sewing trousers and tops in the striped material. Nobody ever checked our work. A guard walked around making sure everyone was working and not taking a break. If you were caught having a rest or talking, the guard hit you very hard on your head or back. One day, a lady argued with the guard who just took a gun out and shot her in the head. Everyone kept looking down and continued to work. The guard ordered two of the women to take the dead woman outside.

One day, the door opened and two of my aunts walked in. It was wonderful to see them again as we had no idea they were at Auschwitz or indeed alive. The last time we saw them was before we went to the ghetto. They were allocated to our hut and they managed to get bunks close to ours. It really was wonderful to have some family nearby again. I remember one sadistic, Latvian woman guard who always seemed to be looking for an excuse to punish prisoners. She saw my Aunt Rebecca taking an unauthorised rest and hit her several times then told her that if it happened again, she would be shot.

Although the food was terrible, we ate everything that was available. People stole food from other prisoners and sometimes fought over a piece of stale bread. Every night people died and in the morning they were removed from the hut. It was such a relief to wake up in the morning and find that we were still alive. I always felt responsible for my sister Rachel, just as she did for me. When we were working, we heard the guards talking about our blue eyes and blond hair, which was just beginning to grow again. Fortunately, they did not realise we could understand what they were saying. They believed that all Jews were stupid and uneducated.

One morning in February 1945, when the snow was on the ground, the SS rounded up several thousand of us, we were told to gather our belongings and to wear as much warm clothing as we could. We managed to find some sacking to tie around our shoes. As we walked out of the camp gates, we thought we were being taken to the forest to be shot, but instead we set off towards Germany, a long line of bedraggled prisoners. The guards were all shouting; they appeared to be even more excitable than usual. They told us the Russians were approaching and it was necessary for us to hurry. If we couldn't keep up we would be shot. We walked and walked, resting from time to time, stopping in barns and outbuildings wherever we could to rest for the night. We collected vegetables from the countryside and ate whatever we could. If anyone became ill or could not walk any further, a guard shot them, leaving them on the side of the road. There was no discussion. They shot one of my aunts, such a tragedy, particularly after she had survived for so long! We heard later that we had left Auschwitz because the guards could no longer exterminate prisoners as they had used all the gas and supplies were no longer getting to the camp.

One morning we awoke to discover that all the guards had left and we were alone in a deserted village, in an isolated area. Most of the prisoners carried on walking west; we were quite exhausted and decided to rest for a while in an abandoned house. It was such luxury, there was a well in the garden and a small pile of old vegetables in an outhouse. It looked as if the owners had just walked out. We assumed that they had fled to the West to avoid the Russians. We managed to make some soup with the vegetables and we collected water from the well. It was the best soup I had ever had.

The next day the Russians arrived, but they were unable to help us as they were pursuing the retreating German army. We remained in the house until we felt stronger, then left and spent several months travelling to Prague, where my mother's relatives lived. It was such a relief when we found them; they had been told that all the family had perished in Auschwitz.

Fortunately, they were Christian and had survived the war. They welcomed us into the family and nursed us back to health. We were all suffering from severe malnutrition and it took several months before we could eat normally. All food seemed to be too rich for our stomachs. My aunt also took some time to recover from tuberculosis. Eventually my sister returned to school. I found I could not concentrate, so took a job in a factory. Sadly, we found out through the Red Cross that we were the only survivors of our family. In fact, very few Jews from our little town survived the Holocaust.

When I was 20, I decided to make the difficult journey to the British zone in Germany to try to obtain a visa for England or America. An official there agreed to help me and he obtained the necessary papers for me to travel. When I eventually landed in Southampton, I realised I needed to learn to speak English and I had to find a job to support myself. From then on, my life changed. The local Jewish community helped and guided me and four years later I went to college and trained to be a primary school teacher. I realised that I had been one of the very lucky ones; I had survived.

I managed to get work locally. I met and married a Jewish man who had spent the war years in England and enjoyed teaching until I retired. I am still in contact with my sister, who lives in Prague.

Sara lives in Hampshire with her husband. She has three daughters and five grandchildren.

Chapter 27

Three short accounts ...

Nicky – 2 years old: Isle of Man

Nicky was nearly 2 years old when war was declared. She lived in Douglas, on the Isle of Man, with her parents and two sisters. She only remembers the last two or three years of the war.

Although the Isle of Man is several miles off the English coast, it is a Crown Dependency and actually pays the British Government for protection. Britain defends the island and, in return, the island agrees to raise a regiment in time of war. My grandfather fought with the Manx regiment in 1918, so it was a mere formality that my father should join as a doctor in 1939.

He was posted to Egypt and wrote letters to my sisters and me every week in the form of a story about a little Egyptian boy; one chapter each week. We watched eagerly for the post to arrive with a new chapter. I still have a copy of this, which is now in the form of a book.

My mother was determined that we should remember my father and she spoke about him every day. His photograph was always on a side table in a prominent position. My grandfather who was a retired doctor came out of retirement to work in the practice. Everyone was keen to contribute to the war effort. Even my uncle who worked long hours as a surgeon at the hospital helped whenever he could.

Life on the island was very relaxed and we seemed to be a long way from the fighting in Europe. However, we were bombed on two occasions. We heard that Liverpool had been the main objective and we had been bombed as a result of a German plane straying from its target. Thankfully there was little damage.

We were told that children in England were starving so the island sent beef, lamb and dairy products to Liverpool. We had a large garden and we grew a great deal of fruit and vegetables. My mother insisted that we should all help with the work. I worked alongside her and she always made me feel my 'work' was valuable. Actually, I may have been more of a nuisance than a help! If she had a surplus of raspberries, apples or plums, she made jam or preserved the fruit for the winter months. She was always so busy. We had ration books and I can remember standing in queues hoping to buy three oranges (one for each child in a family). We also queued for fish and meat and other items in short supply.

When I was 5, I started going to school with my sisters. One day the sirens sounded and my mother ran after us and took us back home. We did not have an air raid shelter but she thought it was better if we were all together with her. Fortunately, it was a false alarm. I do not remember seeing air raid shelters or barrage balloons on the island.

One summer we went on holiday to relatives in Lincoln. While we were there the siren sounded and we all ran into the shelter in the back garden where we remained for two hours. My aunt brought Ludo, Snakes and Ladders, a flask of tea and a cake, which helped us all to relax. This was certainly an exciting experience for us and I will always remember the noise, bangs and thuds. At times the shelter seemed to move. Later we heard it had been a big raid and there had been loss of life. It was in Lincoln that I first saw the large, menacing barrage balloons and the many air raid shelters in the gardens. It was all very different from the Isle of Man. Although we had a good holiday and enjoyed being with our cousins we were pleased to return home where we all felt safe.

Before the war the Isle of Man was a popular holiday venue for holi-daymakers from the mainland and consequently, Douglas had many large Edwardian boarding houses. When the war began the government requi-sitioned these houses and billeted German, Austrian and Italian internees from all over the United Kingdom. These were often people who had lived and worked in Britain since the 1900s and many had been born in Britain. The authorities put barbed wire around the streets where the boarding houses were.

The internees living on the island came from all walks of life. There were teachers, doctors, chemists, plumbers, joiners, restaurant owners, chefs and so many more, before long many of them were contributing to island life. A large number of young men left the island in 1940 with the Manx regiment or they joined the Royal Air Force or the Royal Navy. Many young internees worked on the land replacing the young men who had gone to war. Some made wooden toys of a very high standard and these were sold in local shops at Christmas. On our way to school we often talked to these men and got to know some of them. I am sure they missed their families. These internees were divided into various categories. Some were thought to be a threat to security and these were housed outside the town in a special camp.

My grandfather was very pleased to have the help of an Italian doctor and said he worked well with both island people and other internees. Before the war he had worked in the Italian Hospital in London. Others helped in different ways. We were never frightened of these men who were always helpful and polite. Sometimes wives and children came to visit them and stayed in local boarding houses.

When I started school my mother returned to work as a nurse and she also worked for the Red Cross, she was determined to contribute to the war effort and she needed to be busy.

When VE day finally arrived, the people on the island celebrated with parties, bonfires and fireworks. We then had to wait for my father to return, he had been away for five years. My sisters remembered him, but to me he was a stranger and it took some time for me to accept him. However my mother was so happy and relaxed when he returned.

Before long the internees went back to their families and the island returned to normal. A few actually stayed on the island and married local girls.

Nicky is married and has three children and several grandchildren. She is a retired magistrate.

Aldo – 15 years old: Egypt

When war was declared I was living with my family, on the Island of Gezira. This is an island on the Nile connected to Cairo by a bridge. We lived in Zamalek, which is a beautiful district, very popular with Europeans and middle-class Egyptians.

We heard news from Europe and were aware of what was happening and how Germany was occupying so many countries. We read English newspapers and we heard about the Battle of Britain and how young men flying Hurricanes and Spitfires had fought bravely and stopped the German invasion of Britain. I decided then that I would join the RAF and fly when I was 18.

There had been a British presence in Egypt since the nineteenth century, but in 1922 Egypt became independent. Cairo seemed to be full of British soldiers who lived and worked in the capital They were there to train the Egyptian Army and also to protect the Suez Canal.

When war was declared our lives did not change, at that time it didn't affect Egypt and the Middle East. My brothers and I went to a Catholic school every day at 7.30 am and returned for lunch at 1.30 pm. After a short siesta, we went to either Gezira Sporting Club or the Turf club where we played tennis, swam and relaxed with other Europeans. We stayed there until early evening when we returned home for our evening meal. There was a large British and French community, which was involved with the Suez Canal so we had many friends. My mother had a very easy life; she had a nanny, a cook, and several servants who looked after our house and garden. Whenever we had a birthday in the family or there was an excuse for a celebration, we went to Groppi's to sample the wonderful ice cream, cakes, and little petit fours. Groppi's had been in Cairo for many years and was a favourite with all Europeans.

As the war progressed it was imperative for the British to ensure the safe passages of ships sailing through the Suez Canal; it meant that ships coming from India did not have the long voyage around South Africa. Every morning British aircraft flew up and down the canal deactivating any mines that had been dropped during the night. There were many Commonwealth soldiers in Egypt. Indian Army gunners manned ack-ack guns protecting the Canal.

Many more soldiers came to Cairo for their leave and enjoyed staying in such an interesting city. The soldiers worked and lived in places called Helwan or Heliopolas, where there were army barracks. Many of the officers lived on houseboats on the Nile and most of them worked in the city The Egyptians on the whole accepted them and were pleased to have their custom. The British employed a large number of Egyptians and trained many of them.

Some Egyptians supported and admired the Germans, so when the war in North Africa was at its height and Rommel seemed to be winning these people expected Rommel to enter Cairo and the British to leave. He actually managed to get to the outskirts of Alexandria. Many Europeans were very worried as there was nowhere for them to be evacuated to. I heard one or two discussing a possible evacuation to South Africa. Some Europeans, especially if they were Jewish, went by train to Palestine or the Sudan. When Montgomery took over the Eighth Army and news came of victory at El Alemein with Rommel retreating, there was great rejoicing among the European population. I know my parents were very relieved.

When I reached my eighteenth birthday, I went to England and joined the Royal Air Force and learnt to fly, fulfilling my ambition.

Aldo lives in Strasbourg and is a retired Consul.

Concetta – 14 years old: Island of Ischia, Italy

Concetta was born on Ischia, an island situated off the coast of Naples. The people living there were mainly agricultural workers cultivating grapes, lemons and tomatoes, which grew well on the volcanic soil. Most of the people in the villages and hamlets owned land and grew vegetables and fruit for their own consumption. They kept chickens, goats and pigs and sold any excess produce. This is Concetta's story.

I lived in Porto Ischia, a small town on the coast with my grandmother, parents, my two brothers and an older sister. For me, it was a very comfortable existence; our lives were mainly involved with the family and everyday living. When I was very young, my father was away from home, he had joined the Italian navy and was based in Sardinia.

In 1930, when I was 4 years old he returned to the island and became involved with the wine trade. He went to all the villages, collected the local wine and then exported it to the mainland. Both the white wine and the red wine had a good reputation and was popular. This was a job he enjoyed and we lived a comfortable life.

When Mussolini came to power in the early 1930s, he did many good things. He was very patriotic and his aim was to make Italy a prosperous, successful country, to be admired by the rest of Europe. He created sports stadiums, schools, bridges and roads. He was aware that the population needed to grow, so he encouraged families to have at least five children. As an incentive, he introduced tax concessions for children, an idea that was very new in those days.

We did not have a daily paper, but we listened to the news every day on the wireless. It was years later that we realised that a great deal of what we had been told was propaganda. We heard that Germany had successfully taken back the territory in Poland and Czechoslovakia that had been lost after the First World War. We heard that the German army had been welcomed by the local population. We knew that Italy had invaded Ethiopia and all reports were positive and Mussolini spoke about restoring the former glory of Italy. We just accepted all this, I cannot remember it even being talked about in our house.

Mussolini was a dictator and had secret police, however, the regime was not as strict or as cruel as that of Nazi Germany. Everybody was expected to join the Fascist party and had to carry a party card. My uncle was a lawyer who disapproved of Fascism and refused to join the party, consequently it was impossible for him to get any work.

My brothers and I went to school, where we were required to join the Picola Fascista (little fascists). Boys were told that they would grow up to be warriors and girls were encouraged to be good mothers and homemakers who would provide Italy with the next generation of children, the future of Italy. I left school at 14 and continued my education for the next three years at Economica Domesticos, a domestic science college.

The island had a small contingent of German soldiers billeted on it. They had not come as invaders, they were there to support Mussolini. They established a submarine supply base which refuelled and supplied the submarines with food and munitions. They did not involve the local population, except to buy local produce. However, as time passed and food become short, they simply took whatever they wanted from farmers and people with smallholdings. When it became difficult to import food from the mainland, the black market started and everything became very expensive. From 1942 onwards, we realised that Naples was being bombed by the British. We watched planes flying over us and travelling towards Naples. We could hear bombs dropping and see the flames and smoke coming from the docks. Despite all of this, we still felt safe on our little island, it was as if the war was passing us by. The following day on the radio, the announcer stated that there had been a minor skirmish over Naples the night before. One brave Italian airman had lost his life, whereas at least six enemy aircraft had been shot down. There was no mention of the loss of civilian life or damage to property. Years later, we heard that thousands of civilians had perished in the raids.

Ischia was bombed on one occasion, a house was demolished and a ship called the *Santa Lucia* was attacked and sunk with a large loss of life, mainly young sailors from the island. The ship was bringing supplies from Naples to the submarine base. It was a sad time for families and loved ones.

My father re-joined the navy in 1939 and was posted to Naples as a recruiting officer. He stayed there until 1943 when the Allies landed in the south. When the Italians surrendered, the Germans continued fighting. In several places, the Germans accused the Italians of treachery and even shot some of them as deserters. To avoid being captured and possibly shot, my father and some colleagues took a small boat and rowed back to Ischia overnight. They removed any insignia and buttons off their uniforms and they just melted into the local population. Before long, my father was working once again in the wine industry and we returned to being a normal family again.

In 1943, the young man who was eventually to become my husband landed on Ischia with a British landing force. The Royal Navy arrived one night with tank landing-craft, making as much noise as they could in an attempt to frighten any resistance. What they didn't know was the Germans had already left from the north of the island. There was absolutely no resistance at all!

The local people welcomed the British Navy and Ischia was taken over unopposed. Women and young girls were told to stay in their homes as there was the potential that they could be raped by the invaders. Slowly, people realised that this advice had just been more propaganda and the newcomers were not to be feared. In fact they were friendly, helpful and behaved respectfully towards women.

Smallpox broke out and the British Naval doctor treated local people and vaccinated everyone. The senior Naval officer was Lieutenant Commander Goddard. His remit was to occupy the island, make sure there was clean water, fuel and electricity. He had on his staff an efficient team, each with an area of expertise. He sorted out the fresh water supply, opened up medical centres and set up a transport system. Up until then, people used the fountains in the streets or wells which were all over the island. The local people appreciated what was being done.

My sister had a baby and she was looking for a cot. She was told about an Englishman who was known by locals as Mr Top, the Marischello who had made things for other people. She contacted him on the beach where he had a workshop. He was a naval engineer who had been told to help the local people as much as he could, he came to our house to see what was required. My parents welcomed him and that was how we met. He wondered how old I was as he had seen me around and had wondered how he could make contact with me. That was the beginning of our romance and my future life. He could speak no Italian, but I was lucky to have studied English and French at school. One of my brothers worked for Mr Top as an interpreter. About this time some Americans came to the island and used it as rest and recuperation centre. They brought with them a small band of nurses. My brother had the job of transporting these nurses. They stayed at Casa Micciola.

In our home we used charcoal for cooking. During the war the quality of charcoal was poor and our friend Mr Top made a simple fan which ensured the fire burned well. My mother was the envy of all her neighbours, she thought he was a splendid young man and was happy to see him as a suitor for me. We rarely had any time on our own however, it was arranged that there was always a brother or sister with me. Europe was still at war, but we continued to make plans for our future. This meant leaving the island when the war was over and going to live in the UK. We decided that if we couldn't settle there, we could always return to Ischia. It all seemed very exciting to me.

Dr Halman, the naval doctor interviewed me, there were strict medical checks to make sure I was fit and healthy. He explained the difficulties I could have if we married and went to live in a new country. He also suggested that I was very young, I was just 18 years old. Tom was interviewed by his commanding officer and also by our local priest, who asked him to sign a document to say any children would be brought up as Catholics. All this made us more convinced we were doing the right thing. With everyone's blessing we were married in the Catholic church in Porto Ischia on 10 December 1944. It was such a happy day; we had lots of friends and colleagues around us. My husband had even managed to obtain extra rations to help make it a very special day. The war continued throughout Europe until the following summer. We both moved into my mother's house and stayed there until Tom arranged for me to go to England on a troopship. I made my way to Ramsgate, where I stayed with Tom's family until he returned to England in 1946. Everybody on the ship and in England was kind and welcomed me into my new home. At the end of the war, Dr Halman was given the freedom of Ischia, his family have remained friends to this day.

Concetta lives in Kent; she is a widow with three sons a daughter and many grandchildren.

Chapter 28

A collection of shorter memories

John – 8 years old: London, England

We lived in a pub and our air-raid shelter was at the bottom of a long garden. After a few months of going to the shelter every time the siren sounded, my mother decided it would be just as safe and more comfortable in the cellar as we would also have drinks and crisps on hand.

Joy – 6 years old: London

We had a spare bedroom and my mother took in a lady who was a milliner. She came up with the idea to make slippers. She brought back skins in all colours; they lined them with butcher's muslin. They were in great demand and people ordered them by size and colour. It was a very successful enterprise.

Kath – 4 years old: Wales

My parents ran a café and guest house; this was requisitioned by the government to be used as a military clinic. We only had a few days to leave and find some rented accommodation.

Pat – 7 years old: Bedford, England

One thing I remember was that all our village name signs were taken down. The finger posts pointing towards nearby towns and villages were removed and even the sign on our village hall was painted out. Our post office was renamed 'Village Post Office'.

Our school started to produce school dinners. This was to help working mothers to do war work. The meals were not brilliant, but I think they were nutritious and usually consisted of a stew-like meal with potatoes and vegetables, followed by a milk pudding or a tart.

Jenny – 11 years old: England

On VE and VJ day I went with my family to London and we stayed at the Cumberland Hotel. There were great celebrations with fireworks, bonfires and lots of music. It was a very joyful time. Everyone was cheering and dancing. People were talking to strangers and enjoying the moment.

Christine – 11 years old: England

I cannot remember any anti-Jewish feeling. We had a family of Austrian Jews living nearby. The father and the boys had travelled by train from Germany to Switzerland then on to England. They were very clever and worked hard. When they first came to England they could not speak English. Two years later they passed their school certificate and eventually went to University.

David – 7 years old: Portsmouth, England

We returned to Portsmouth and in the evening we went up to Portsdown Hill. The old underground tunnels built under the hill were used as shelters; we went into them, taking food and flasks of tea. We slept on bunks fitted inside the tunnel. In the morning, we would return to our house and hope that it had not been bombed during the night.

An Anderson shelter was built in our garden. One night we went into it as bombs were falling in the area. When the 'All Clear' sounded, we went back into the house and found firemen with buckets and stirrup pumps putting out fires in the bedrooms. Some incendiary bombs had gone through the roof and one had penetrated the ceiling and set my mother's bed on fire.

Wendy – 7 years old: England

We had two young evacuees from London billeted in our house. Although they were lively, they were well behaved and polite. One day, when a German plane crashed near our village, they went looking for souvenirs. A few days later the local policeman questioned them and found that, among other things, they had a box full of live ammunition!

Christine – 14 years old: England

We really enjoyed VJ Day. I was working at a Farming Camp at the time. We were given time off school to help with the potato and sugar beet harvest.

It was hard work and some farmers did not pay and were unpleasant. Thankfully, most of them were kind and appreciated what we did and paid us. In the evening we went to the local youth club and had lots of fun singing, dancing and watching a firework display.

Colin – 8 years old: London, England

One night during a raid, we heard several doodlebugs flying over, this was followed by an enormous explosion which really shook our shelter. The vibration was dreadful and the whole thing seemed to move. When we emerged we found that one had landed close by and completely demolished a whole line of houses. There was debris and glass everywhere. People just stood and looked at the mess and then they tried to help the ARP rescue any survivors.

Epilogue

After nearly six years of war, on 8 May 1945, war in Europe came to an end and VE day was declared. Three months later, VJ day was celebrated and then the Second World War was over. On both days, people in Europe and in the United Kingdom celebrated with parties. In the UK, there were street parties, dancing in the streets and sports events. Tables and chairs were brought out and everyone got together to celebrate with sandwiches, cakes and food. Rations for sugar and flour had been saved for such an occasion. Bonfires blazed, some in the middle of roads, church bells rang, flags appeared and from nowhere, fireworks filled the sky. In London and other towns and cities, street lights came on. It was difficult to believe it was all over; everyone seemed happy and relieved, talking, laughing and dancing with complete strangers. In the Channel Islands, people celebrated with the soldiers who had liberated them.

For many families, peace brought problems with it. Soldiers, sailors and airmen returned home, many of them like strangers to their wives and children. Some children resented these 'strangers' coming into their homes, telling them what to do. With the men being away for so long, many women had become independent and some marriages never recovered. The scars of war took a long time to heal.

Houses, shops and schools destroyed by bombing had to be rebuilt and in some areas, prefabricated buildings were erected for a time. Some remained in use twenty years later and it took a while for people to believe that the war really was over.

Children continued to receive milk every day at school. Cod liver oil and orange juice were available at a small cost. Rationing continued for several years and children were disappointed because they thought that their rationed sweets would return to the shops more quickly than they did.

During the war years, children in Britain were, on the whole, well cared for. Rationing ensured they had a healthy diet at low cost. Although many experienced a disrupted education and sleepless nights due to bombing and being separated from loved ones often inflicted emotional scars, which these took a long time to heal. The Channel Islands were the only part of the UK that was occupied by the Germans and their children experienced the same hardships as other occupied countries.

In continental Europe, people celebrated being free once again although, in some countries, life was difficult for quite some time. In Germany, there was a shortage of food, water and electricity and it was not possible to transport supplies into the towns and cities. Germans had to accept that it was they who were now the occupied country and they were no longer the 'Master Race'.

This was the time for retribution. Those who had acted against their own people were asked to account for their actions. Some were arrested, some were imprisoned and some were executed. Young women who had collaborated with the enemy had their heads shaved.

During the war, in an occupied country, children had to be careful what they spoke about outside the home and could not always be sure who they could trust. They knew that that a knock on the door could result in a loved one being taken away and sent to an internment camp or to work in an enemy country many miles away. At times, they were starving and some witnessed events that an adult should not witness, let alone a child.

Children all over Europe grew up in spite of difficulties and deprivation. This book is their story. I hope I have given justice to their experiences.

Glossary

Agenda: The agenda in Greta's story was the diary that her father wrote recording his actions once the Norwegian royal family had escaped. This diary is in the museum in Elverum in Norway. There are drawings showing how they blew up the bridges and railways.

Ack-ack guns: Slang for anti -aircraft guns.

Air raid shelters: The Anderson shelter was the most common. Three and a half million shelters were built at the beginning of the war. They consisted of cylindrical sheets of corrugated iron placed over a hole dug into the ground. The hole was at least 4ft deep. In this 'hole' there were usually benches to sit on and people tried to make them as comfortable as possible. The top of the shelter was covered with a thick layer of soil or turf. Unfortunately, they often had a tendency to flood in the winter months.

- **Morrison Shelter:** This was a shelter built inside the house. It looked like a large box and could be used as a table. The whole construction was reinforced and was designed to protect people from debris and falling masonry.
- **School shelters:** Once war was declared, children were not allowed back to school until shelters had been built. Some were brick built on the surface but some were underground. There were benches to sit on and a blast wall in front of the entrance.
- **Public Shelters:** Some of these were brick built with concrete roofs and were built in streets and could accommodate a large number of people. The underground in London was also used as a shelter. People went down at night and stayed there till morning, taking with them blankets and pillows.

Annexation of Sudetenland: In September 1938, France, Britain, Italy and Germany signed the Munich Pact which allowed Germany to take back the Sudetenland. This was part of Czechoslovakia where three million ethnic Germans lived. It also handed over Czech coal iron ore and seventy per cent of the electricity. Germany marched into Czechoslovakia and took over the country. It became one of the Nazi's most avid supporters of the third Reich.

Aryan: Hitler and the Nazis considered anyone who was pure German to be of Aryan stock. The antithesis of Jewish or Romany ancestry. They would check a person's lineage and, if in doubt would research back three generations.

Autobahn: German motorway built in 1938.

Auschwitz: Nazi concentration camp in Poland.

Baedeker Raids: The Baedeker Raids were a series of destructive raids against historic cities and towns in Britain. It was thought that they were as a reprisal for RAF raids on Lubeck and Rostock.

Bailiff of Guernsey: The office of Bailiff is given to the senior judge on the island. He is the presiding officer of the Royal Court, a really important position on the island.

Band Iron: iron strips usually used in plumbing and heating.

Barrage Balloon: These were large balloons filled with hydrogen, attached to a steel cable. The balloons were raised and lowered by a large winch. This ensured that enemy aircraft had to fly higher and their bombing would be less accurate. They were used over British towns, ports and harbours and were very effective.

Belsen: A Nazi concentration camp near to the town of Celle in Northern Germany.

Berlin Air lift: After the war, the Allies (United Kingdom, France, America, and Russia) partitioned the city of Berlin. Berlin was deep in the Russian Zone. On June 15 1948, the Russians closed all roads, canals and railroads from Western Occupied Germany into the city, to the three allied sectors. For more than a year the Allies ferried provisions by air from Western Europe into Berlin Templehof, Gatow and Tegal airports, and a lake in Berlin. The Allies sent 2.3 million tons of cargo in the airlift. The Blockade was lifted in 1949, that was when NATO (North Atlantic Treaty Organization) was created.

Blackout: In the UK in 1940, a blackout measure was introduced. Streetlights were turned off and from sunset until sunrise it was illegal to show even a chink of light from any house or building. People made curtains from heavy black material. Torches had the top half of the glass obscured. Kerbs, trees and lampposts had a white band painted around them. All car headlights had to be specially modified.

Black market: This was an illegal trade in rationed or scarce goods, which people sold for profit 'on the black market'.

Blitz: A term used to describe German bombing of British cities, but it is more commonly used for the bombing of London. Many cities suffered a great deal of damage and loss of life, among them Coventry, Liverpool and Hull, but of course many other cities suffered a great deal of damage and loss of life.

SS *Blucher*: This was the first German ship to be sunk by the Norwegians in Oslo fjord. It was the flagship of the German invading forces.

Bunkers: Air raid shelters for town and city people in Germany. Most were underground and were large. People spent their nights in these shelters. Hitler and the German High Command had their headquarters in a bunker in Berlin.

Burnt Earth Policy: This is usually referred to as 'Scorched Earth Policy' and was a military strategy carried out by the Germans in Eastern European countries and in Norway. It involved destroying anything that might be of military use to an approaching army, for example houses, barns and transport. This tactic was also used by the Soviet forces.

Clothes Rationing: Clothes ration started in 1941. Children were issued with more coupons than adults, this was to take into account that children grew out of clothes. Coupons were needed for knitting wool, but parents often unravelled a jumper and used the wool again.

Crown Dependency: Guernsey, Jersey and the Isle of Man are Crown Dependencies. They are not part of the United Kingdom, but have a relationship with the Commonwealth. They are recognised as 'territories' for which the United Kingdom is responsible. The monarch is represented by a Lieutenant Governor on the Isle of Man and in Jersey and Guernsey by a Bailiff. They have their own currency, but they recognise and accept the currency of Britain. They are British citizens. Britain is responsible for the defence of the islands.

Curfew: In occupied countries, the Nazi regime imposed hours of curfew. This was usually between 8pm until 8am. No one was allowed out during that time. If caught, severe punishment would be imposed unless one had a very good reason; needing a doctor for example.

D-Day: Day of the Normandy landings.

Demilitarisation of Guernsey and the Channel Islands: At the beginning of the war, the British Government realised that they would not be able to defend the Channel Islands once France was occupied. In the First World War, the Channel Islands were demilitarised. In 1940, thousands of children were evacuated to Britain. When the Germans arrived they were surprised to find here were no British troops on the island. The Bailiff stated to the Germans that Guernsey was an 'open island', with no armed forces.

Dig for Victory: Growing one's own food was called 'Digging for Victory'. Any spare ground, gardens or allotments were used. This was a great help to the country.

Doodlebug: Term used to describe the V1. This was an unmanned flying bomb.

Evacuees: Evacuation was not compulsory, but thousands of children left their homes to stay in a safer place, living with local families in the country. In some cases, teachers went with them.

Food rationing: Food rationing started in 1940. The first items to be rationed were butter, bacon and sugar, but very soon more items were included. Offal, meat pies, sausages and fish were not rationed. It was designed to give fair shares to all.

Gasmasks: Gas masks were issued to both adults and children and they were kept in cardboard boxes. Babies were given special bags. At school, children had to practice putting them on every day. Many children hated the wearing of a gas mask.

Gulags: Internment/concentration camps in Siberia and Russia.

Hedgerow Harvest: In the summer holidays children collected the 'hedgerow harvest'. This involved collecting wild fruit, nuts, sphagnum moss, and other medicinal plants, especially rose hips, The WVS paid collectors three pence for a pound in weight of this valuable harvest.

Hershey bars: American chocolate bars.

Inches: An imperial unit of length, approximately 2.5cms.

International Red Cross: The International Red Cross covers Swedish and British Red Cross. It was a neutral organisation that helped both sides in the war. It signed the Geneva Convention.

Internees: These were German, Austrian and Italians men who had lived in the United Kingdom pre-1939. They were sent to the Isle of Man for the duration of the war. They were divided into different categories for security. Some actually worked on the island.

Kinder: German word for child.

The SS *Viga*: A Swedish ship that took supplies to the Channel Islands. It was based in Lisbon and actually saved the lives of many Channel Islanders. The food parcels came from Canada and New Zealand. The Swedish Red Cross sent food parcels to Norway and to Rotterdam when the local population was starving.

Milk Ration: In 1940, the National Milk Scheme was introduced and children under 5 received a pint of milk each day. Children in school received half a pint of milk a day. Extra milk was allocated to all children under 18.

Morse code: System of dots and dashes used to send messages.

Nissen Huts: Prefabricated steel structure made from a half cylinder skin of corrugated steel. They were used to house soldiers.

Orange distribution scheme: In 1941, whenever oranges were available these were given to people with a green ration book (a child's ration book.) People were limited to three oranges or the equivalent of a pound in weight, usually one orange per child was allowed.

PoW: Prisoner of war.

Quisling: Vidrun Quisling was the Norwegian politician who supported the Nazi regime; his followers were called Quislings. After the Norwegian king left for England, he was elected Minister President by parliament. Quislings were regarded as traitors by most Norwegians. He was executed at the end of the war.

Ration books: At the beginning of the war ration books were issued, a buff colour for adults and a green one for children under 6. In 1941, a blue ration book was issued to children over 6, who received extras such as cod liver oil and milk. There were also ration books for clothing.

Razzias: This was the term used in the Netherlands, during the Nazi occupation, to cover raids on houses looking for young men to be sent to Germany to work in factories, to help the German war effort.

Scrip: This was the currency used on Jersey, during the occupation, by the Germans.

Smart Alec: Colloquial term similar to 'know it all' or 'smarty pants'.

Star of David: In Germany and every occupied country, the Nazis insisted that Jews should wear a yellow star on their clothes. It was to ensure that a Jew could be easily identified.

Slave labour: The Germans brought labour to the Channel Islands to build fortifications on the islands and railway lines. Most of these people lived in poor conditions, but were paid and fed. However, they brought Russian and Ukrainians prisoners, who were regarded as *untermenschen*, ie 'subhuman'. These poor people were treated dreadfully and were beaten and starved before eventually dying. Many islanders helped these people, but if caught were sent to concentration camps.

WVS: Women's Voluntary Service.

VE Day: Victory in Europe, 8 May 1945. The whole of the country celebrated and the street lights were turned back on.

VJ Day: Victory against Japan, 15 August 1945. The Second World War was finally over.

Acknowledgements

I would like to thank everyone who contributed their stories so willingly; from the U.K. to diverse countries in Europe, stretching from the Soviet Union to Malta, Norway, Italy and beyond. They were all very happy to share their amazing wartime experiences, and without them, I would not have been able to write this book.

A special thank you to Nadia, whose dramatic story inspired me to compile this set of wartime memories. Thank you also to my daughter, Nessa, who tirelessly read the scripts, correcting punctuation. To Adam, a big thank you for his help with ICT. Thanks must also go to my husband, Derek, who kept me going with tea, coffee and encouragement.

I would like to express my gratitude to Mike and Anne-Marie Edwards, both experienced authors, who gave me such good advice at all stages of the writing process.

Index